# The Rembrandt House
*the prints, drawings*
*and paintings*

# The Rembrandt House

## *the prints, drawings and paintings*

Eva Ornstein-Van Slooten

Marijke Holtrop

Peter Schatborn

Translated by Harry Lake

Waanders Publishers - Zwolle

Museum Het Rembrandthuis - Amsterdam

# *Table of contents*

page 2
Museum Het Rembrandthuis,
Interior of the 'Sijdelcaemer'.

# *Preface*

The first extensive descriptive catalogue of the Rembrandt prints and drawings in the collection of the Rembrandt House, written by J.P. Filedt Kok, appeared in 1972. Because that book has now been out of print for several years it was decided to publish a new complete catalogue. The present volume contains slightly less detailed descriptions, but it does present illustrations of all the works in the collection. The authors are indebted to Dr Filedt Kok for his permission to draw freely on his texts in the first catalogue. They have made grateful and sometimes word-for-word use of them.

The Society of Friends of the Rembrandt House Museum has been closely and enthusiastically involved with the project at all stages and is bearing some of the cost: the museum is much indebted to them.

We should like to thank Mr Hidde Hoekstra for his critical reading of all texts and Ms Charlotte ten Holder for the perfectionism with which she has made the text ready for the printer. Despite the usual shortage of time they have given their assistance cheerfully and unflappably.

Mr H.S. Lake is responsible for the English translation and Mr R. Taylor has taken new photographs of the entire collection: we thank them both for their collaboration.

We are grateful to the publishers, Waanders, and the staff who worked on the production of this book, for the accommodating and pleasant way in which they have liaised with us: we hope that they, like us, will be satisfied with the result of our joint efforts. Finally, we hope that this catalogue will enable many visitors to the museum to look at the Rembrandt House collection through different eyes.

The authors

# History of the house and collection

The year in which the Rembrandt House was built, 1606, falls within Amsterdam's period of richest blossoming. Expanding trade was attracting numerous immigrants and the city's population was to double to c. 100,000 in the first quarter of the century. After earlier urban expansions, in the major enclosures of land to the east and south-east of the city in 1593 a large new area was brought within the city walls. This new part of the city was bisected by the St. Anthoniesdijk, later called the Breestraat, which - after the construction of the St. Anthoniessluis in 1606 - was quickly built over. On the corner of the Zwanenburgwal and the Breestraat Hans van der Voort had two houses built: the corner house he moved into himself, the second, on the Breestraat, he sold to the wine merchant Pieter Belten, a native of Antwerp. At this time the ring of canals round the city had yet to be dug, and the new neighbourhood centred on the Breestraat was much sought after by wealthy merchants.

The map of the city by Balthasar Florisz. of 1625 tells us what the house looked like when it was built: an L-shaped plan, an in those days exceptionally wide facade with four architraves, and a stepped gable that began just above the first floor (pl. I). This was probably replaced in about 1633 under the direction of the painter-architect Jacob van Campen (architect of the Mauritshuis in The Hague and the Palace on the Dam in Amsterdam) by the present gable, a triangular corniced pediment. This added an extra floor to the house and gave it a modern appearance (pl. II). On 5 January 1639 the heirs of Pieter Belten sold the house to Rembrandt for 13,000 guilders, payable in instalments. By this time there had already been some decline in the prestige enjoyed by the neighbourhood. When Rembrandt moved in, his next-door neighbour on one

pl. I
Detail from the map by Balthasar Florisz., dated 1625. In the middle the house Rembrandt bought in 1611.

page 6
Museum Het Rembrandthuis, Interior of the entrance-hall.

pl. II
Pediment and cornice on the facade of the Rembrandt House.

pl. III
The Rembrandt House before the restoration
that lasted from 1908 till 1911.

large studio. Rembrandt had his studio at the front of the house and at the back he had a room for his collection of art and curiosities. The inventory gives a breathtaking list of the collection, which also spilled out into other parts of the house. For almost twenty years, a considerable portion of his working life, this was the house in which Rembrandt lived and worked. But in 1656 financial problems, including the matter of paying off the purchase price of the house itself, forced him to apply for *cessio bonorum*. That is to say, he surrendered all he owned to be sold for the benefit of his creditors. The inventory was drawn up and in 1657/58 both house and contents were sold. Rembrandt moved to a house (no longer standing) on the Rozengracht (nowadays no. 184), where he lived until his death. Shortly after his departure, in about 1660-2, the house on the Breestraat was divided vertically into two separate houses. Gradually the whole character of the neighbourhood began to change, with increasing numbers of shops and small businesses. The varied succession of occupants of the Rembrandt House, whose names we know from documents in the archives of the city, ended in 1906, three hundred years after Rembrandt's birth. From within the committee formed to coordinate the celebrations of this tercentenary, there came a call - initially from the painter and etcher Jozef Israels - for a more worthy use to be found for the building that had been Rembrandt's home for so long. This suggestion met with warm approval and before the year was out the city of Amsterdam had purchased the house from the Spits brothers, who had a shop selling clocks and haberdashery in the left-hand half of the building and let the right-hand half divided into several flats.

In 1907 the Rembrandt House Foundation was established and purchased the house from the city. The famous architect K.P.C. de Bazel was brought in to restore it. Inside the house the original arrangement had been completely lost in a succession of alterations. Nor was there much left in the facade, with its nineteenth-century windows and double entrance, to recall the original situation (pl. III). It was decided that the stepped gable should not be restored but that the raised front with the pediment should be retained. The windows were replaced by cross windows and instead of the double entrance there came a single entrance door. Inside, the inventory of 1656 and the traces of old joisting, wall joints etc. discovered during the work were used to restore the original arrangement as far as possible. To enable the house to be used as a museum, stairs were installed where the original 'small office' had been. This also meant the loss of part of the antechamber to the art room on the floor above. For the exhibition rooms de Bazel designed panelling, display cases and other furniture. In 1911 the restoration was complete and on 10 June of that year the museum was officially opened by Queen Wilhelmina.

At the suggestion of the painter Jan Veth, one of the members of the museum's first board of governors, it had already been decided to assemble a collection of Rembrandt's etchings, which, it was felt, could hardly be better displayed than in the house in which most of them were made.

Veth himself laid the foundations for the collection with the temporary loan of those etchings in the Lebret-Veth collection that were of sufficient quality. The first gifts were not long in coming. In the same year Jonkheer J.F. Backer, secretary to the board of governors, presented the museum with its first

side was Salvador Rodrigues, a Portuguese Jewish merchant, and on the other the portrait painter Nicolaes Eliasz (Pickenoy). The art-dealer Hendrick van Uylenburgh, Saskia's uncle, lived on the corner of the Breestraat and the Zwanenburgwal. Diagonally across the road from Rembrandt lived the writer and printer Manasseh ben Israel, who was also rabbi of the Beth Israel synagogue on the Houtgracht behind Rembrandt's house.

We know little about the interior of the house when Rembrandt lived there. The only clue is the inventory drawn up in 1656, after Rembrandt's declaration of insolvency. Here the contents of the house are described room by room. The clerk began his tour of inspection in the main room of the front part of the house, moved from there into the side room, again facing the street, then on into the room behind that and finally into the large room in the rear part of the house, which also seems to have served as a bedroom. Four rooms are mentioned on the first floor: the 'art room', its anteroom, the small studio and the

drawing: *Esau selling his birthright* (cat. 8, pl. IV). Backer had bought it as a 'Rembrandt', but it is now ascribed to the school of Rembrandt. From Paul Warburg in New York came the first gift of an etching: a fine early impression of *St. Jerome beside a pollard willow* (cat. B 103, pl. V). Still in the same year Jozef Israels gave the new museum six etchings including *Abraham's sacrifice* (cat. B 35) from the famous English collection of W. Esdaile. An honorary member of the board of governors, Jonkheer P. Hartsen, deserves a special mention. His generous donations, having helped make the purchase of the house possible in the first place, then continued to add to the buying fund. The Rijksmuseum donated eleven etchings, doublets from the print room which have been in the Rembrandt House ever since.

The collection grew rapidly: here, of course, there is room only to mention some of the outstanding items.

In May 1913 thirty-three Rembrandt drawings were auctioned in Amsterdam from the famous English collection of J.P. Heseltine. The Rembrandt House succeeded in acquiring four of these: *Seated girl, sleeping* (cat. 6), *Woman with a child on her arm* (cat. 1), *The ruins of the old Town Hall in Amsterdam* (cat. 4) and the *View of the Montelbaenstoren in Amsterdam* (cat. 3).

At other sales too the Rembrandt House bid successfully. In 1914 Veth returned from Berlin with nineteen etchings, including such important pieces as *Death appearing to a wedded couple* (cat. B 109), *The large lion hunt* (cat. B 114) and - to bolster the then still poorly represented landscapes - a fine impression of the *View of Haarlem and Bloemendaal* (cat. B 234).

The war years that followed brought a temporary end to the growth of the collection, though in 1915 the foundation was able to buy sixty-six etchings from the collection of Jan Veth,

pl. IV
Unknown pupil of Rembrandt, *Esau selling his birthright*. This is the first drawing that was donated to the Rembrandt House in 1911.

most of which were already in the museum on loan. They included some beautiful and rare prints, among them *The flight into Egypt*, on a plate by Segers (cat. B 56) and *David and Goliath* (cat. B 36c), designed as an illustration for Manasseh ben Israel's book *Piedra Gloriosa* (Amsterdam 1655). In 1927 the Rembrandt House was to acquire, as a gift from I. de Bruyn, one of the extremely rare copies of the first edition of this mystical work, including Rembrandt's four illustrations. Other items to come from the Veth collection were an early, heavily inked impression of the fourth and final state of *The three crosses* (cat. B 78b) and the beautiful little portrait of *Rembrandt's mother* (cat. B 351).

The museum's collection of drawings was also growing, albeit slowly. In 1919 two sheets came from the estate of Thérèse van Duyl, who had bought them at the Heseltine sale: the *Portrait of an old woman* (cat. 9) and the study of a *Woman with a child on her arm* (cat. 7), now attributed to Nicolaes Maes. Not long afterwards another drawing from the famous Heseltine sale, the portrait of the artist in his painting coat (cat. 5), was purchased. This meant that the museum now had the only drawn full-length self-portrait. Until 1741 the sheet had been in the possession of the famous French collector Pierre Crozat, who had probably acquired it from the collection of Roger de Piles. He, in turn, may have bought the drawing when he was in Holland in 1693.

pl. V
Rembrandt, *St. Jerome beside a pollard willow.*
The first etching donated to the Rembrandt
House in 1911.

In 1925 Jan Veth, the museum's enthusiastic driving force, died. His successor on the board of governors was the collector I. de Bruyn, who was largely to assume Veth's role as an adviser. By this time the collection had already become extremely large. But there were lacunae, mainly in the often rare early dated prints, e.g. the self-portraits and studies of beggars.

In February 1933 a further six etchings were bought at the Houthakker/Hollstein sale, though the threat of war was already becoming painfully apparent. Directly after the invasion of May 1940 the etchings and drawings were moved into the safe in the cellar. When the city threatened to be flooded in the spring of 1944 the works of art were moved to a safer location above ground in a bank safe, where they remained until after the liberation.

The museum reopened in July 1945. This was followed by a number of lean years. Lack of funds and a shortage of supply meant that few purchases of any note could be made. But in 1950 the museum was able to buy a counterproof of the fourth state of *The three crosses* (cat. B 78c): an interesting addition to the states of the print already in the museum's possession. The most important postwar acquisitions are the forty etchings bequeathed to the museum by de Bruyn, who died in 1962. These included the very rare first state of the *Self-portrait with bushy hair* (cat. B 8), a fine impression on Japanese paper of *Christ and the woman from Samaria* (cat. B 70), from the collection of Pierre Mariette, an early, heavily inked pull of *The descent from the cross by torchlight* (cat. B 83) and a beautiful first state of *The bathers* (cat. B 195).

It was becoming increasingly difficult to fill the gaps in the collection. Good copies came onto the market only sporadically and even then the funds with which to purchase them were often lacking - hardly surprising in view of the way prices have risen. Occasionally something could be added, as in 1977, when

a drawing by Rembrandt's pupil Constantijn van Renesse, with corrections by Rembrandt, was purchased with the help of the Vereniging Rembrandt (cat. 12). Other additions have been in 1980 the etching *Man at a desk, wearing a chain with a cross* (cat. B 261) and, very recently, the little *Bald-headed man in profile (Rembrandt's father?)* (cat. B 294).

Thus the collection in the Rembrandt House, assembled over a period of over eighty years through private initiative and with private funds, has now grown into an almost complete survey of Rembrandt's graphic work.

Museum Het Rembrandthuis, Interior of the 'Agtersael'.

# The technique of etching

Abraham Bosse, *A printer's workshop*.
Etching, 1642. Museum het Rembrandthuis.

The chemical technique of etching was developed in the Middle Ages by Arabic armourers as a means of applying decoration to weapons. It flourished in the fifteenth century in south Germany, where the first etched prints on paper were printed towards the end of the century.

During the first decades of the seventeenth century Dutch artists like Esaias van de Velde, Jan van de Velde II and Willem Buytewech experimented with the technique. They were looking for greater tonality and an atmospheric effect in their landscape prints and tried to achieve this by breaking up the long contour lines into short strokes and dots.

Hercules Segers experimented with etching for a different reason: he tried to produce a painterly effect by printing on coloured paper or canvas, also working up his prints afterwards with a brush in colour and thus incidentally making every impression unique.

Rembrandt must have taken more than a little interest in these developments, for he ultimately took the technique to extremes even more than had his predecessors. In his hands, etching

became a fully fledged medium which occupied him at intervals for the rest of his life. This resulted in an oeuvre of some 290 etchings, all intended as substantive works of art. Rembrandt's masterly use of the drypoint and the unique deep black of many of his etchings were famous even in his own day and his work was much sought after by the many print collectors of the time.

What follows here is a description of the technique of etching, with details of its use in Rembrandt's work. The etchings in the Rembrandt House collection cited as examples are described in the catalogue section.

Prints are impressions, usually on paper, of designs fixed by the artist on some kind of medium, by drawing, painting or cutting. The medium may be a wooden block, a plate of metal, or a silk screen. One of the techniques used for making prints is etching. Here the medium is a thin copper plate. This is covered with an acid-resistant mixture known as the etching ground, composed of asphalt, resin and wax. Into this thin covering the design is drawn with an etching needle, so that where the needle penetrates the etching ground the copper is exposed.

We know that Rembrandt used a fairly soft, pasty etching ground of his own devising. This allowed him to draw the design in a free, loose manner. The extent to which he was sometimes able to approach the sketch-like effect of a pencil or crayon drawing in his etchings is seen in cat. nos. B 114, B 195 and B 208. Rembrandt almost always drew his design straight onto the plate. True, he often drew preliminary studies on paper, but these were used only as a guideline. It was very rare for him to transfer the design of such a study onto the etching ground, as in cat. nos. B 201, B 271 and B 285.

Example of etched lines.

The plate is then laid in a bath of dilute acid. The exposed parts that are no longer protected from the acid by the etching ground - that is, the lines of the design - are etched away, producing grooves in the surface of the metal. The longer the plate is left in the bath, the deeper these grooves become. If particular lines have to be deeper than others, the plate is removed from the bath, the lines that have been bitten deeply enough are covered with acid-resistant stop-out varnish, and the plate is replaced in the bath.

Rembrandt used a dilute solution of hydrochloric acid. This worked slowly and did not make thin lines coarser.

Example of drypoint lines.

Now the etching ground is removed and the clean plate inked with an ink-pad or roller. It is then wiped clean by hand so that the whole plate is clear of ink except for the grooves.
The next step is to lay a damp sheet of paper on the plate. Then plate and paper are passed through the rollers of the press. The paper absorbs the ink from the grooves, producing a reversed impression of the design on the plate. The lines that have been bitten the deepest, which therefore contain the most ink, come out darkest in the print.
This process is etching proper. Gradations in the lines can be achieved only by etching the plate more than once. However, there are also other ways of producing variation in the density of lines. The most common are working up with the drypoint and burin, drawing directly onto the copper plate.
The drypoint is an etching needle with a sharp point strong enough to carve lines in the copper. As it passes through the copper the drypoint throws up a burr which retains additional ink when the plate is wiped. This makes the printed line slightly ragged or fuzzy. This velvety effect is quickly lost as the plate is used because the burr quickly wears under the pressure of the press.
The burin, which is really an engraving tool - hence its other name, graver - has a V-shaped point which cuts a sharp-edged line starting and ending in a point.

Example of lines made by a burin.

Rembrandt's first plates were pure etchings, i.e. made without recourse to the drypoint, which he initially used only occasionally for small additions or corrections. From about 1640 he became increasingly interested in the painterly effects of the velvety drypoint line: fine examples are to be seen in cat. nos. B 40 and B 103. As a result he started using the drypoint more and more often, sometimes in combination with the burin. Some of his prints, indeed, are executed exclusively with the drypoint, being drawn straight onto the copper (cat. nos. B 76 and B 78).

If the artist is dissatisfied with the result he can alter the etched plate in a variety of ways. He can add or deepen lines by etching the plate again or by using the drypoint, but etched lines can also be erased: shallow ones by rubbing them with a burnisher so that the burr and the sides are pushed into the groove, deep ones by scraping with a scraper. Each change or addition to the plate that can be seen in a print is referred to as a new 'state' of the print. Thus state V (8) means the fifth state out of a total of eight.

Almost all Rembrandt's etchings exist in more than one state, sometimes as many as ten or more. Often the changes are slight, amounting to little more than minor additions or corrections. Sometimes they are so drastic that the result is virtually a new composition (e.g. cat. nos. B 76 and B 78).

Only a limited number of impressions can be 'pulled' from an etching plate. The maximum is probably around a hundred; only about fifteen in the case of a drypoint plate. By the same token, prints of the same state may vary considerably as the plate and the burr become worn.

Prints were still being made from many of Rembrandt's plates at the end of the seventeenth century and even until well into the eighteenth. To disguise the fact that the plates were worn they were reworked. A good example of this practice in the Rembrandt House is the series cat. B 74 b-f. Comparatively few of Rembrandt's plates have survived. A batch of 78 plates owned in the eighteenth century by the French printer and engraver J.F. Basan are now in an American collection on loan to the museum in Raleigh, N.C. A number of loose plates also exist, among them the plate for the portrait of Jan Six (cat. B 285), which is still in the Six collection in Amsterdam.

It is also possible to introduce deliberate variation by inking the plate differently. The artist can leave more or less ink in the grooves to obtain a correspondingly darker or lighter impression.

Examples of very lightly inked prints which look almost like silverpoint drawings (the silverpoint is just that: a silver point held in wood like the lead in a pencil. It was used on paper prepared with an opaque white coating) include cat. nos. B 58 and B 96. In prints like our cat. B 78b, by contrast, Rembrandt achieved a very dark effect by inking the plate heavily.

One can also deliberately not quite wipe the surface of the plate entirely clean, leaving a little ink on it instead. This produces a greyish haze over the impression. This is called 'surface tone'.

Rembrandt used surface tone principally to give greater depth to shadows, as in cat. nos. B 86, B 107 and B 202, and occasionally to produce an atmospheric effect in his landscapes, as in cat. nos. B 223 and B 228.

Different types of paper (e.g. European, Japanese and 'Chinese') and vellum (made from animal skins) vary in colour and surface structure. This can be exploited to good effect. The same plate printed on different papers could produce totally different impressions.

From about 1650 Rembrandt sought increasingly to introduce variation into his prints by using different sorts of paper. Japanese paper, which was actually imported from Japan, attracted him with its warm, yellowish colour, which was particularly effective in prints of Italianate landscapes such as cat. nos. B 70, B 104 and B 107. Moreover with its fine, smooth surface Japanese paper does full justice to the drypoint work. Many of Rembrandt's prints were done on Japanese paper. Particularly noteworthy examples are cat. nos. B 94, B 123 and B 197.

A counterproof is a reversed print made by taking a freshly made print when it is still damp, laying a blank sheet of paper on it, and passing both sheets through the press. This produces a print of a print - the counterproof - which naturally, being reversed twice, corresponds exactly to the original design on the plate. Useful to the artist wishing to make minor adjustments to the plate.

A fine example of a counterproof in the Rembrandt House collection is that of the fourth state of *The three crosses* (cat. B 78c).

# *Biography*

| | |
|---|---|
| 1606 | Rembrandt Harmensz van Rijn born in Leiden. |
| 1620 | Rembrandt is enrolled at the university of Leiden after several years at the Latin school there. |
| end 1620/ early 1621 | Rembrandt leaves the university and becomes apprenticed to Jacob Isaacz van Swanenburg, a Leiden painter. |
| 1623-24 | Apprenticeship to the history painter Pieter Lastman in Amsterdam. |
| 1624 | Rembrandt returns to Leiden where he has his own studio. He also collaborates with Jan Lievens. |
| 1631 | Rembrandt moves to Amsterdam, where he lodges in the house of the art-dealer Hendrick van Uylenburgh. |
| 1634 | Rembrandt marries Saskia van Uylenburgh, a niece of Hendrick van Uylenburgh. |
| 1635 | Their first child is born, a son Rumbartus, who dies within two months. Rembrandt and Saskia move to the Nieuwe Doelenstraat. |
| 1638 | Birth and death of a daughter, Cornelia. Members of Saskia's family accuse Rembrandt of squandering her property. |
| 1639 | Rembrandt and Saskia buy a house on the Breestraat, now the Rembrandt House Museum. |
| 1640 | Birth and death of a second daughter, Cornelia. |
| 1641 | The second edition of Jan Orlers's *Beschrijvinge der stadt Leyden* (Description of the city of Leiden) is published. It contains the first printed biography of Rembrandt. |
| 1641 | Birth of a son, Titus. He survived into adulthood. |
| 1642 | Death of Saskia after a long illness. A nanny, Geertge Dircx, moves into the house to look after Titus. *The Night Watch* is completed. |
| 1648 | Geertge Dircx, now Rembrandt's mistress, makes a will in which she leaves her entire estate to Rembrandt's son Titus. |
| 1649 | Hendrickje Stoffels makes her appearance in Rembrandt's household, supplanting Geertge Dircx. Geertge Dircx sues Rembrandt for breach of promise. Rembrandt's financial position worsens. |
| 1650 | Rembrandt has Geertge Dircx committed to a lunatic asylum. |
| 1654 | The church council accuses Hendrickje of 'whoredom' with Rembrandt. Birth of a daughter to Rembrandt and Hendrickje, Cornelia. |
| 1656 | Because of his enormous debts Rembrandt applies for *cessio bonorum* (the surrender of his property). This puts the settlement of his debts in the hands of the court for insolvent estates. An inventory of Rembrandt's property is taken. |
| 1657 | Rembrandt's possessions are sold at auction. |
| 1658 | The house on the Breestraat is auctioned, but Rembrandt and his family are allowed to stay there for a further two years. |
| 1660 | Rembrandt, Hendrickje, Titus and Cornelia move to a house on the Rozengracht. Titus and Hendrickje form a partnership in order to do business in the art trade. (Following the public sale of his property Rembrandt is banned from operating independently in the art market.) |
| 1663 | Hendrickje dies. |
| 1665 | Titus receives his part of the proceeds of the auction of 1657-8. |
| 1668 | Titus marries in February and dies in September. |
| 1669 | Titus's daughter Titia is born in March. Rembrandt dies on 4 October and is buried in the Westerkerk in Amsterdam on 8 October. |

Detail cat. B 76a.

# Drawings

**1**

*Woman with child on her arm*
Pen with brown ink, 104 x 87 mm
Benesch 342; Filedt Kok 1972, no. III

The woman with the child on her arm was probably originally part of a larger sheet, the sketches on which have been cut into separate drawings so as to increase the dealer's profit. The women and children portrayed by Rembrandt were not always members of his own family: three of his four children died young and only Titus survived into adulthood. The drawings done in the 1630s were probably inspired by the family of Hendrick van Uylenburgh and his wife Maria van Eck, in whose house Rembrandt lodged at the beginning of his Amsterdam period and who in 1634 had six children. In the inventory of Jan van de Capelle of 1680 the drawings of these models are recorded as '...135 drawings of the life of women with children...'

This drawing must have been done at the same time as a sheet in the Fondation Custodia (F. Lugt collection) in Paris (Benesch 343), on which the same figures are shown, with a child behind the skirts of the woman playing peekaboo with the child in her arms. The drawings date from the mid 1630s.

**2**

*Figure studies*
Black chalk, 133 x 231 mm
Benesch 373; Filedt Kok 1972, no. IV

The type of the old woman with the stick appears in an etching by Rembrandt entitled *The Spanish gypsy Preciosa* (B 120), which is generally dated *c.*1642. Rembrandt quite often drew sketches like this in black chalk. In some of them the woman carries a child on her back, as in the etching of *Beggars receiving alms at the door of a house* (B 176).

Although this sheet of sketches is generally dated *c.*1637 it was more probably executed in the 1640s. There is another sketch of the same old woman (Benesch 737) which was executed at about this time and has been linked with the *Preciosa* etching, and there are other small drawings of comparable figures or groups. The unusual thing about the sheet in the Rembrandt House is that it has not been cut into smaller drawings.

**3**

*View of the Montelbaenstoren in Amsterdam*
Pen and brush with brown ink, on several
pieces of paper pasted together,
145 x 144 mm
Benesch 1309; Filedt Kok 1972, no. V

Not far from Rembrandt's house stood, as
it still does today, the Montelbaenstoren,
originally part of the city fortifications. To
the right, beyond the tower, we see a
rowing boat and behind that a wooden
palisade extending straight on from the
end of the quay. To the left of this is
where an artificial island called
Waalseiland was created in 1644-6. This
too still exists today. In front of the ship in
the background is another palisade
extending across the entire width of the
drawing. Like the other one, it has been
executed with the pen and a light brown
wash. Above the rowing boat there is an
opening. These palisades are a recurrent
feature of seventeenth-century maps.
If the drawing is topographically accurate,
it was made before the island was created.
A map of Amsterdam dating from 1647
shows the island, though at that time it
had probably not yet been built on. The
drawing of the Montelbaenstoren is
generally dated later, *c.*1650, but the
evidence of the map would seem to
indicate that it was actually executed
before about 1647. Rembrandt
deliberately omitted the modern conical
roof by Hendrick de Keyser which had
decorated the tower since 1606. Evidently
he wished only to show the old part of the
building, just as he had omitted the new
roof from a drawing of a tower called
Swijgh Utrecht (Benesch 1334), which was
also part of the old city defences. In this
way the towers became 'historical'
buildings as we see them in the Biblical
scenes, e.g. in the background of the
etching *The agony in the garden* (B 75).

**4**

*The ruins of the old Town Hall in Amsterdam*
Pen and brush with brown ink, touches of
red chalk, 150 x 201 mm
Bottom right, in Rembrandt's hand: *vand
waech afte sien stats huis van Amsterdam/ doent
afgebrandt was/ den 9 Julij 1652/ Rembrandt
van rijn.*
(The town hall of Amsterdam after it was
burnt down on 9 July 1652, seen from the
weighing house)
Benesch 1278; Filedt Kok 1972, no. VI

Three days after the fire which destroyed
the old town hall Rembrandt drew the
ruins, also documenting the event with a
caption. The demolition of a number of
houses to make way for a new town hall
behind the old one had begun in
December 1646 and the first pile for the
new building was driven on 20 January
1648.
An undated drawing by Rembrandt in
black chalk (Benesch 1275, plate 4A),
made from the Nieuwezijds Voorburgwal,
shows the situation before the fire, when
the demolition work at the back of the old
town hall was already far advanced.
However, there is no sign there of the new
building such as may be seen on a print in
the atlas of Frederik Muller (no. 2031) in
the print room of the Rijksmuseum, from
which it appears that at the time of the fire
in 1652 two storeys had already been
completed. The drawing in black chalk
was thus presumably made sometime
between 1646 and 1648.
In the left foreground of the 1652
drawing there is a wooden shed with a
canvas tent roof and leaning against the
ruined building are the ladders used in
fighting the fire. Shortly after the fire the
tower was pulled down because it was in
danger of collapsing.

plate 4A
Rembrandt, *The old Town Hall in Amsterdam, seen
from the Nieuwezijds Voorburgwal,*
Vienna, Albertina.

**5**

*Full-length portrait of Rembrandt*
Pen with brown ink on brownish paper,
203 x 134 mm
Bottom centre: *getekent door Rembrant van
Rhijn naer sijn selves/ sooals hij in sijn
schilderkamer gekleet was* (Drawn by
Rembrandt van Rhijn of himself as he was
dressed in his studio.)
On the cardboard mount, in the
handwriting of P.J. Mariette: *Rembrant
avec l'habit dans lequel il avoit accoutumé de
peindre.*
Benesch 1171; Filedt Kok 1972, no. I

According to the inscriptions, both of
them old but not contemporaneous with
the drawing, Rembrandt has drawn
himself dressed in his painting jacket and
wearing the hat also seen in the etched
self-portrait of 1648 (B 22). In a painting
now in Vienna (Bredius 42) he wears the
same jacket and holds his hands to his
sides in the same way. The painting bears
the date 1652, which is the approximate
date given to the drawing.
The inscription in French is by the
connoisseur and art-dealer Pierre-Jean
Mariette and was probably written on the
occasion of the Pierre Crozat auction of
1741, the catalogue for which was
prepared by Mariette. The Dutch
inscription is probably older, but the
identity of its author is unknown.
The figure has been rather sketchily
drawn, with a few powerful, dark accents.
The right foot can be seen in two different
positions and the paper has been
damaged at the belt, probably when an
excess of ink was erased.

**6**
**Willem Drost** (active 1650-1670)
*Seated girl, sleeping*
Pen and brush with brown ink,
139 x 99 mm
Benesch 1104; Filedt Kok 1972, no. II

When it was in the collection of Valerius
Röver in 1739 this drawing was
considered to be a Rembrandt, but since a
clearer picture has emerged of the oeuvre
of Willem Drost, one of Rembrandt's
pupils, an attribution to him has seemed
more plausible. Characteristic of Drost's
style is the profuse and varied hatching,
the lines of which sometimes flow together
to form broader areas, and his
occasionally broad contours.

**7**
**Nicolaes Maes**
(Dordrecht 1634 - 1694 Amsterdam)
*Woman with a child on her arm*
Pen with brown ink, 89 x 41 mm
Verso: *Sketch of a hand*
Red chalk, 89 x 41 mm
Filedt Kok 1972, no. VIII;
Sumowski VIII, no. 1885

Following Rembrandt's example his pupil
Nicolaes Maes made many paintings and
drawings of women and children. Maes
was working in Rembrandt's studio in
about 1650 and this small sketch was made
at the beginning of the decade. The sketch
in red chalk on the back shows that the
drawing was once part of a larger sheet.

**8**
**Unknown pupil of Rembrandt**
*Esau selling his birthright*
Pen and brush with brown ink,
190 x 265 mm
Benesch 607; Filedt Kok 1972, no. VII

Esau, seated on a chair in the middle, has
returned exhausted from the chase and
extends an arm to take the bowl of soup
(the Biblical 'mess of pottage') offered him
by his brother Jacob in exchange for his
birthright. Esau wears a knife at his waist
and his hat lies on the table; behind him
we see his hunting dog.
This drawing was formerly attributed to
Rembrandt but is now regarded as the
work of a pupil or imitator of the early
1650s. Rembrandt himself drew the same
subject in the 1640s (Benesch 606), but in
that drawing Esau is depicted standing as
a hunter.

**9**
**Unknown pupil of Rembrandt**
*Portrait of an old woman*
Pen and brush with brown ink,
108 x 93 mm
Filedt Kok 1972, no. IX

This drawing consists principally of
brushwork: there are only a few places
where a pen seems to have been used.
Whether this is an autographic work is still
a matter for debate, but it is unlikely. The
precision of the drawing and the
abundance of brushwork are not
characteristic of Rembrandt. The dating
too is problematical: while 1635-40 is
commonly cited, a later dating in the
second half of the 1640s is more probable.

**10**

**Unknown pupil of Rembrandt**
*Head of a young girl*
Verso: *Head of a sleeping woman*
Pen with brown ink, 91 x 71 mm
Benesch 313a; Filedt Kok 1972, no. XI

This head of a girl has been executed with considerable caution and in fine pen lines, which is why attribution to Rembrandt is doubtful. The sketch of the sleeping woman on the back is conceived in the same style but then elaborated with powerful strokes of the pen. Even so, these strokes do not have the shaping power with which autographic drawings by Rembrandt are imbued, witness for example the hatching and shadows in the neck.

**11**

**Pieter Lastman,** copy after-,
(Amsterdam 1583 - 1633 Amsterdam) *The angel leaving Tobit and his son*
Black chalk, brush with brown ink, heightened with white, 350 x 530 mm
Benesch 474; Filedt Kok 1972, no. X

This drawing was once erroneously regarded as a design for a painting by Rembrandt's teacher Pieter Lastman (Copenhagen, Statens Museum). It was also claimed that Rembrandt was responsible for the black chalk trees in the background.
The whole sheet is now considered to be a copy by an unknown artist, even the contribution by Rembrandt no longer seeming quite so convincing as was once thought. Certainly he did make one or two drawings after compositions by his teacher, but the style of the additions in black does not necessarily reflect that of Rembrandt. This and other copies after Lastman are an indication of the popularity of his historical scenes.

**12**

**Constantijn Daniel van Renesse**
(Maarssen 1626 - 1626 Eindhoven)
*King Josiah and the prophet Hilkiah*
Pen and brush with brown ink,
heightened with white, 185 x 265 mm
Benesch 1379a; Sumowski IX, no. 2202**

Here we see an episode from the story of
King Josiah, who has bidden the high
priest Hilkiah to come to him, Hilkiah
having found the book that lies on the
table to the left, from which a scribe is
reading out the law (2 Kings 22:12-13).
The scene has also been interpreted as
*The prophet Gad gives David the choice of his
punishment* (2 Sam. 24:10-11).
The drawing is one of a group of Biblical
scenes by van Renesse which were
corrected by Rembrandt. His powerful

pen strokes and accents reinforce the
forms and enhance the sense of depth. It
is possible, however, that his pupil then
further elaborated his own drawing in the
manner of his master's corrections: not all
the dark pen lines clearly betray the hand
of the master.
Other drawings by van Renesse were
corrected by Samuel van Hoogstraten,
another of Rembrandt's pupils. In his
'Inleyding tot de Hooge Schoole der
Schilderkonst' (Introduction to the High
School of Painting, 1678, p. 192) van
Hoogstraten advises teachers to improve
their pupils' drawings by sketching 'on the
same object', a practice that he had
evidently learned from Rembrandt.

# *Paintings*

**I**
**Pieter Lastman** (1583-1633)
*Christ on the cross*, 1616
Oil on canvas, 90,5 x 137,5 cm
Bottom centre, on the cross:
PL (monograph) 1616

Pieter Lastman was born in about 1583, probably in Amsterdam, where he died in 1633. In about 1623 or 1624 Rembrandt became apprenticed to Lastman, who at that time was considered one of the most important skilful of all the history painters.

The painting decipts the Crucifixion of Christ at Golgotha, 'the place of the skull'. In accordance with the events as related in the Bible, standing by the Cross are Mary the mother of Christ, Mary Magdalene and Mary the mother of James and Joseph. To left and right of Christ we see the two criminals who were crucified with him (Matt. 27: 33-56; John 19: 17-30). Lastman painted several Crucifixions, but this is the only one to show Mount Calvary.

**II**
**Pieter Lastman** (1583-1633)
*The mourning over Abel,* 1624
Oil on panel, 67,5 x 94,5 cm
Centre right, on the plinth:
PLastman fe/ 1624

Genesis chapter 4 verse 8 relates the slaying of Abel by his brother Cain. The scene depicted here, however, is the mourning of Abel, about which the Bible tells us nothing. It is based on an apocryphal commentary to Genesis. The dead Abel lies propped up against a boulder. On the left of the panel we see Eve wringing her hands, Adam kneeling behind her. On the right, a ram and some sheep - a reference to Abel's occupation as a shepherd.
(C. and A. Tümpel 1970; A. Tümpel 1974)

## III

**Gerbrandt van den Eeckhout** (1621-1674)
*Abraham entertaining the three angels,* 1655
Oil on canvas, 68 x 73,5 cm
Bottom left: G.V. Eeckhout fec/ 1655

Gerbrandt van den Eeckhout was
apprenticed to Rembrandt in about 1635-
40. His biblical pieces betray the influence
of Rembrandt particularly strongly. This
scene depicts Genesis 18: 8, which relates
how Abraham offered the three angels a
meal. It was more common to illustrate a
later point in the story: the moment at
which the angels informed Abraham and
Sarah of the forthcoming birth of their
son (Gen. 18: 9-11).

**IV**
**F.A. Marienhof,** active around 1650
*St. Peter's liberation from the prison*
Oil on canvas, 25 x 35,5 cm

King Herod Agrippa I had Peter arrested
and imprisoned in a dungeon. The night
before his trial Peter slept, bound in
chains, between two soldiers. Two sentries
guarded the door to the dungeon. Then
an Angel of the Lord appeared tot Peter
in a shining light. Peter's chains fell from
him, and the Angel commanded him to
gird himself, bind on his sandals, and
follow him (Acts 12: 3-9).

**V**
**Esaias van der Velde** (1591-1630)
*The reconciliation of Esau and Jacob*
Oil on panel, 67.5 x 122 mm
Bottom right: E VVELDE

The scene is the reconciliation of Esau and
Jacob as related by Genesis 33. Esau,
dressed as a Roman warrior, embraces his
kneeling brother Jacob. On the right of
the panel we see some of the four
hundred men with whom Esau had gone
forth to meet Jacob.
Kneeling behind Jacob are his slaves with
their children, behind them his first wife
Leah and her children, and behind her his
second wife Rachel with her son Joseph.
The quarrel between the two brothers had
arisen out of the episiode of the stolen
blessing, when Jacob tricked his father
Isaac into blessing him instead of Esau
(Genesis 27).

**VI**
**Johan Martinus Anthon Rieke**
(1851-1899)
*View of the Rembrandt House in Amsterdam,*
1868
Pencil, pen with brown ink and
watercolour, heightened with white,
34,6 x 19 cm
Bottom right: A Rieke/1868

At this time the house was divided
vertically into two, as it had been since
about 1660, with two front doors and two
doorsteps.

# *Etchings*

Acknowledgements of authors cited in the
catalogue entries:

**B** numbers refer to:
A. Bartsch, *Catalogue raisonné de toutes les
estampes... Rembrandt...*, 2 vols, Vienna
1797.

**Bartsch** numbers refer to:
A. Bartsch, *Le peintre-graveur*, 21 vols,
Vienna 1803-1821.

**Benesch** numbers refer to:
O. Benesch, *The drawings of Rembrandt*, 6
vols, London and New York 1953-1957;
revised edition by Eva Benesch, London
and New York 1973.

**Gersaint** numbers refer to:
E.F. Gersaint, *Catalogue raisonné de toutes
les pièces qui forment l'oeuvre de Rembrandt*,
Paris 1751.

# *Self-portraits*

Rembrandt is unparalleled as a maker of self-portraits: the painted works continue to the end of his life but the etchings - with one or two exceptions - cease in about 1640. A large proportion of these self-portraits were made in 1628-30, when Rembrandt was living and working in Leiden. They are all in small formats and show only the head or at most a bust. Sitting in front of the mirror Rembrandt would experiment in recording a variety of facial expressions on the plate. He would use studies like these as exercises for the figures that were to express particular emotions in larger compositions. He also used the etchings to study the play of light on his face.

Most of the prints are signed with the monogram RHL (Rembrandt Harmensz Leidensis) which he used up to about 1632. After that, he generally signed his name in full: Rembrandt.

**B 1**
*Self-portrait with curly hair*, c. 1630
Etching, state II (2), 56 x 49 mm
Right centre: RHL

**B 2**
*Self-portrait, wearing a cap*, c. 1634
Etching, only state, 49 x 44 mm

**B 8**
*Self-portrait with bushy hair*, c. 1631
Etching, state I (6), trimmed to
63 x 66 mm

**B 10**

*Self-portrait, frowning,* 1630
Etching, state III (3), 72 x 60 mm

**B 14**
**Rembrandt and pupil**

*Self-portrait, wearing a fur cap,* 1631
Etching and burin
State III (3), 62 x 56 mm
Top right: RH 1631

The only extant examples of this print
were made after the plate had been
worked up by one of Rembrandt's pupils,
probably J.G. van Vliet.

**B 16**

*Self-portrait in a fur cap,* 1631
Etching, only state, 63 x 57 mm
Top left: RHL 1631.

**B 316**

*Self-portrait in a cap, laughing,* 1630
Etching, state V (6), 48 x 43 mm
Top left: RHL 1630

The plate in this state has been
reworked by another hand
(J.G. van Vliet?).

**B 320**

*Self-portrait, open-mouthed,* 1630
Etching, only state, 51 x 46 mm
Bottom centre: RHL 1630

**B 17**
*Self-portrait in a cap and scarf,* 1633
Etching, state II (2), 132 x 104 mm
Bottom left: Rembrandt f. 1633.

**B 19**
*Self-portrait with Saskia,* 1636
a) Etching, state I (3), 104 x 95 mm
b) Etching, state III (3), 104 x 95 mm
In both top left: Rembrandt. f./ 1636

In this double portrait Rembrandt has
depicted himself drawing, or possibly in
the process of making an etching. Beside
him sits his wife Saskia van Uylenburgh,
whom he had married two years earlier.
In the third state a number of minor slips
have been corrected.

**B 18**
*Self-portrait with raised kris,* 1634
Etching and drypoint
State II (2), 124 x 102 mm
Top left: Rembrandt f./ 1634

Here Rembrandt poses in extravagant
attire: he wears a brocade mantle with a
collar of ermine and a cap with an ostrich-
feather, and holds a kris. These are exotic
clothes such as we find listed later in the
inventory of Rembrandt's estate, and he
was fond of dressing both himself and his
models in them. Other examples of such
costumed portraits are B 20 and B 23.

plate 21A
Rembrandt, *Sketsch after Rafael's portrait of Baldassare Castiglione,* Vienna, Albertina.

**B 21**
*Self-portrait,*
*leaning on a stone sill,* 1639
Etching and drypoint
State II (2), 205 x 164 mm
Top left: Rembrandt f./ 1639

Here Rembrandt has depicted himself as a *grand-seigneur.* The striking pose - body in profile, face turned towards the spectator and left arm resting on a balustrade - is borrowed from 'Ariosto' in the portrait by Titian (London, National Gallery). At the time, this painting was in Amsterdam, where it was part of the collection of Alfonso Lopez. While he worked on this etching Rembrandt would also almost certainly have had Raphael's famous portrait of Baldassare Castiglione in mind. That painting was auctioned in Amsterdam in 1639, when it too was acquired by Lopez. Rembrandt did a sketch of it on that occasion (Benesch 451, plate 21A).
Perhaps here he is competing against the Italian masters, demonstrating his equality with them. A year later he made a painted version of this portrait (Bredius 34, London, National Gallery).

**B 20**
*Self-portrait in a cap with plume,* 1638
Etching and drypoint
Only state, 134 x 104 mm
Top left: Rembrandt. f/ 1638
Since 1911 on loan from the
Rijksmuseum, Amsterdam

**B 23**

*Self-portrait with plumed cap and sabre*, 1634
Etching and drypoint
State II (3), 130 x 108 mm
Bottom right: Rembrandt/ f. 1634

Although the likeness is not immediately obvious, this is still a self-portrait. The bizarre clothes and the small number of prints made (only 4 in the first state) would be unlikely in a commissioned portrait. In the first state this was a three-quarter length portrait. In this second state the plate has been cut back to an oval bust.

**B 22**

*Self-portrait, etching at a window*, 1648
Etching, drypoint and burin
State V (5), 160 x 130 mm
Top left: Rembrandt f 1648
Printed on Chinese paper

In this last of Rembrandt's etched self-portraits we see the artist sitting at the window in his working clothes. From the slope of the working surface and the way in which he grasps the tool it would seem that he is in the process of etching.
In this final state, seen here in an eighteenth-century impression, the plate has undergone major reworking by another hand, to the extent that a complete landscape has been added.

**B 24**

*Self-portrait, wearing a fur cap*, 1630
Etching, state IV (4), 62 x 52 mm
Top left: RHL 1630

**B 26**

*Self-portrait, wearing a flat cap*, c. 1642
Etching, only state, 93 x 62 mm
Signed: Rembrandt f.

# *Biblical scenes*

Biblical subjects from both Old and New Testament account for a large proportion of Rembrandt's work. He depicted some of his favourite subjects several times in paintings, drawings and etchings. Examples include the vicissitudes of Abraham and Tobit and scenes from the youth of Christ such as the flight into Egypt and Christ disputing in the temple.

In his Biblical prints Rembrandt followed not only the text but also, more importantly, the pictorial tradition. In almost all of them it is possible to recognize themes inspired by earlier depictions. He drew very freely and creatively on the work of his predecessors, which he would have known well from his own large colection of prints (which included over 3,000 sheets of Biblical subjects alone).

Rembrandt. f. 1638.

**B 28**

*Adam and Eve,* 1638
Etching, state II (2), 162 x 116 mm
Bottom centre: Rembrandt. f. 1638

After the creation Adam and Eve lived in the Garden of Eden. Their time in paradise came to an end when Eve was seduced by the serpent into eating the forbidden fruit of the tree of knowledge of good and evil (Gen. 3:1-24).
Adam and Eve are depicted very realistically as ordinary, naked, no longer particularly young people. The serpent (borrowed from a print by Dürer, Bartsch 16) is a monster with claws. According to the Bible the animal did not have to crawl over the ground on its belly until after the Fall.

**B 29**

*Abraham entertaining
the three angels*, 1656
Etching and drypoint
Only state, 159 x 131 mm
Bottom left: Rembrandt f. 1656

The three angels are being entertained by
Abraham, to whom they promise that his
wife Sara, already well on in years, will
soon bear a son (Gen. 18:1-15). At the
front we see the guests sitting round the
table. Beside them stands Abraham, jug in
hand. In the doorway Sarah listens
disbelievingly. The boy with the bow and
arrow is Ishmael, Abraham's son by
Sarah's maid Hagar (see also B 30).
The composition is broadly similar to that
of a drawing done by Rembrandt at about
the same time (Benesch 1187) in which he
copied a Mogul miniature of 1627/28
showing four sheiks in conversation.

**B 30**

*Abraham casting out Hagar and Ishmael,*
1637
Etching and drypoint
Only state, 125 x 95 mm
Top right: Rembrandt/ f 1637

When her marriage failed to produce any
children Sarah sent Abraham her
bondservant Hagar, who subsequently
bore him a son, Ishmael. Eleven years
later Sarah herself bore a son, Isaac, upon
which she forced Abraham to send Hagar
and Ishmael into the desert. Although
their situation seemed hopeless, they were
later saved by God (Gen. 21:1-21).
This story, particularly the dramatic
moment of Hagar's departure, was one of
Rembrandt's favourites and was also
popular with his pupils.

**B 33**
*Jacob and Benjamin*, c. 1637
Etching and drypoint
State II (2), 116 x 89 mm
Bottom left: Rembrandt f.

**B 34**
*Abraham and Isaac*, 1645
Etching and drypoint
Only state, 157 x 130 mm
Bottom left: Rembrandt/ f. 1645.

To test Abraham, God demanded of him
that he sacrifice his son Isaac. When they
arrived at the place which God had
appointed, Isaac asked in his innocence
where the lamb was that was to be the
burnt offering. Abraham replied that God
would provide it (Gen. 22:1-8).

**B 35**
*Abraham's sacrifice*, 1655
Etching and drypoint
Only state, 156 x 131 mm
Bottom right: Rembrandt f. 1655.

The sequel to the events in the preceding
print is depicted in this etching, made ten
years later. Just as Abraham made to slay
his son an angel came between the two
because God was sufficiently convinced of
Abraham's obedience (Gen. 22:9-14).
The compactness of the central group
makes it stand out against the background
as if sculpted.

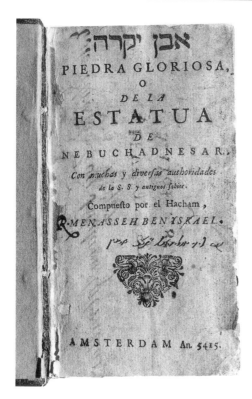

**B 36**
Manasseh ben Israel
*Piedra Gloriosa o de la Estatua de Nebuchadnezzar*, Amsterdam 1655

This little book, written in Spanish by Manasseh ben Israel (see also B 269), is a mystical treatise on the coming of the Messiah. Manasseh constructed his story round the 'glorious stone, hewn not by human hand' (Dan. 2:34), a symbol of the Messiah. He used this stone, the *Piedra Gloriosa*, in all four of the themes illustrated.
This copy is one of the four remaining books containing the illustrations by Rembrandt discussed below (B 36a-d).

**B 36a**
*Nebuchadnezzar's dream*, 1655
Etching, burin and drypoint
State III (5), 96 x 76 mm
Bottom left: Rembrandt f 1655
Printed on vellum
Since 1911 on loan from the Rijkmuseum, Amsterdam

The image with feet of clay and iron that Nebuchadnezzar saw in his dream was shattered by a stone 'cut out without hands' (Dan. 2:31-5). This stone, the 'glorious' stone of Manasseh's title, would later fill the entire earth. Rembrandt makes a reference to this in the globe on the right.

**B 36b**
*Jacob's ladder,* 1655
Etching, drypoint and burin
State II (3), 106 x 69 mm
Bottom left: Rembrandt f 1655
Printed on Japanese paper
Since 1911 on loan from the
Rijksmuseum, Amsterdam

The same stone referred to above served
Jacob as a pillow when he slept and
dreamed of a ladder stretching to heaven,
with the angels ascending and descending
it (Gen. 28:11-15).

**B 36c**
*David and Goliath,* 1655
Etching and drypoint
State IV (5), 106 x 74 mm
Bottom left: Rembrandt. f. 1655

Here Rembrandt shows us the moment at
which David makes ready to sling the
stone that will kill Goliath (1 Sam. 17:49).
In Manasseh's interpretation this is the
same stone as in the preceding episodes.

**B 36d**
*Daniel's vision of the four beasts,* 1655
Etching, drypoint and burin
State II (2), 99 x 76 mm
Bottom left: Rembrandt f 1655
Printed on Japanese paper
Since 1911 on loan from the
Rijksmuseum, Amsterdam

In his apocalyptic dream Daniel saw four
monstrous beasts rise up out of the sea.
Then the Ancient of Days (i.e. God)
appeared to him dressed in a garment as
white as snow, seated upon a throne. The
beasts were destroyed and eternal
dominion was given to 'one like the Son of
Man' (Dan. 7).
It is curious that Manasseh, a rabbi,
should have had no objection to this
etching: Jewish law prohibits all images of
men and certainly of God.

**B 37**

*Joseph telling his dreams*, 1638
Etching and drypoint
State II (3), 110 x 83 mm
Bottom left: Rembrandt f./ 1638

Joseph, his father Jacob's favourite son, aroused the jealousy of his brothers. Their hatred for him grew stronger still when Joseph told of a dream from which it could be deduced that they would one day all make obeisance unto him (Gen. 37:1-11). The brothers' angry reactions to this story are depicted with vigour and conviction.

This print was preceded by a detailed grisaille study in oils (Bredius 504, plate 37A) and various preliminary drawings of individual figures.

plate 37A
Rembrandt, *Joseph telling his dreams*, Amsterdam, Rijksmuseum, Rijksprentenkabinet.

**B 38**

*Joseph's coat brought to Jacob*, c. 1633
Etching and drypoint
State I (2), 107 x 80 mm
Bottom right: Rembrant/ van. Rijn. fe.

Joseph's brothers sold him into slavery, dipping his coat of many colours into the blood of a young goat and telling Jacob, their father, that they had found it in the desert. Jacob, understandably believing that Joseph had been torn to pieces by wild beasts, was inconsolable (Gen. 37:31-34).

**B 39**

*Joseph and Potiphar's wife*, 1634
Etching, state II (2), 90 x 115 mm
Bottom left: Rembrandt f. 1634.

Sold into Egypt as a slave, Joseph became the trusted servant of Potiphar, captain of the guard at the court of the Pharaoh. Potiphar's wife attempted unsuccessfully to seduce him. In the scene shown here Joseph has just succeeded in freeing himself from her clutches: but she has held onto his coat and will later use it as evidence when she falsely accuses him of trying to seduce her (Gen. 39:7-12).

**B 40**

*The triumph of Mordecai*, c. 1641
Etching and drypoint
Only state, 174 x 215 mm

The book of Esther describes the vicissitudes of the Jews in exile in Persia in about 475 BC. One of them, Mordecai, discovered a conspiracy against King Ahasuerus, who was married to Mordecai's foster-daughter Esther. When the king wished to express his gratitude he asked his adviser Haman - a fierce opponent of the Jews - what should be done for the man whom the king wished to honour. Haman, assuming that he himself was to be the recipient of this reward, suggested that the man be dressed in the king's clothes and led through the city on the king's horse. The king immediately ordered him so to do with Mordecai (Esther 6:6-12).

Here Rembrandt shows us the triumphal procession in honour of Mordecai. In the top right of the picture we see King Ahasuerus and Queen Esther watching from a balcony.
At about this time (1641/42) Rembrandt was also engaged on the Night Watch. Signs of this can be seen in this etching: in the architecture, for example, or in the composition and the chiaroscuro. Some of the individual figures are borrowed from the engraving of the same title by Lucas van Leyden, and another source of inspiration was the painting by Rembrandt's teacher Pieter Lastman (now on loan to the Rembrandt House from the Rijksdienst Beeldende Kunst).

**B 41**
*David in prayer,* 1652
Etching and drypoint
State I (3), 143 x 93 mm
Bottom centre: Rembrandt f. 1652.

**B 42**
*The blindness of Tobit,* 1651
Etching and drypoint
State I (3), 160 x 129 mm
Bottom centre and bottom right:
Rembrandt f. 1651

The Apocryphal book of Tobit (known in
Dutch as Tobias) served as a source of
inspiration to Rembrandt and his pupils
on many occasions. Here we see the
moment at which the old, blind Tobit
hears his son returning and hurries to the
door. In his haste he knocks over the
spinning wheel; his dog tries to guide him
and leaps about by his feet.

## B 43

*The angel departing from the family of Tobit,*
1641
Etching and drypoint
State II (4), 103 x 154 mm
Bottom centre: Rembrandt f 1641

This scene from the story of Tobit follows
on from that shown in the previous print.
Tobit's son Tobias has returned from his
long journey. His travelling companion
and consellor - to whom he owes the
recommendation of fish gall as a cure for
his father's blindness - has just revealed
himself as the archangel Raphael and
flown away.

Tobias and his father kneel in the left
foreground. To the right we see the
valuables they offered Raphael as a
reward. The ass in the background would
have been part of the caravan with which
Tobias returned home. The unusual
image of the angel flying away is
borrowed from a woodcut after Maarten
van Heemskerck (Hollstein 49, plate 43A).
Rembrandt was evidently impressed by
the way Heemskerck had depicted the
flight of the angel: he had already taken it
as his model when painting the same
subject in 1637 (Bredius 503).

plate 43A
D.V. Coornhert after Maarten van Heemskerck,
*The angel departing from the family of Tobit,*
Rotterdam, Museum Boymans-van Beuningen.

**B 44**
*The angel appearing to the shepherds*, 1634
Etching, burin and drypoint
State II (3), 262 x 218 mm
Bottom right: Rembrandt f. 1634
Since 1911 on loan from the
Rijksmuseum, Amsterdam

In the night there appeared to the
herdsmen in the field an angel who
brought them the tidings of the birth of
Christ. 'And suddenly there was with the
angel a multitude of the heavenly host
praising God, and saying, Glory to God in
the highest, and on earth peace, good will
toward men' (Luke 2:8-14).
The herdsmen and their beasts, scattering
in terror at this apparition, are tiny figures
in the grandly conceived landscape.
Rembrandt has fully exploited the
dramatic contrast between the light in the
sky and in the foreground and the
surrounding gloom of the night.

**B 45**
*The adoration of the shepherds:*
*with the lamp*, c. 1654
Etching, state I (2), 105 x 129 mm
Bottom centre: Rembrandt f.

After the announcement of the birth of
the Messiah the shepherds went to
Bethlehem, where they found Joseph and
the Virgin and the newborn child in the
crib (Luke 2:15-16). The simple,
spontaneous manner of etching is well
suited to the intimate nature of the scene.
This print, with B 47, 55, 60, 63 and 64,
probably belongs to a series about the
youth of Christ: these sheets, all in almost
exactly the same format, add together to
make a thematic and stylistic whole.

**B 46**
*The adoration of the shepherds:
a nightpiece*, c. 1652
Etching, drypoint and burin
State V (8), 148 x 198 mm
Since 1911 on loan from the
Rijksmuseum, Amsterdam

For the subject of this print see B 45.

**B 47**

*The circumcision in the stable,* 1654
Etching, state I (2), 94 x 144 mm
Top left: Rembrandt f. 1654.
Top centre: Rembrandt/ f. 1654.

Eight days after the nativity Christ was
circumcised and given the name Jesus
(Luke 2:21). The Bible does not tell us
where the Circumcision took place.
However, the books of the Apocrypha
situate the scene in the stable, since
according to Jewish law for forty days
following the birth a mother is impure
and may not enter the temple. Despite
this, in western iconography the event
generally takes place in the temple where
the high priest performs the circumcision.
This is also how Rembrandt depicts it in
two much earlier prints (Gersaint 48 and
B 48).
This print is part of the series about the
youth of Christ referred to in the
commentary to B 45.

**Gersaint 48**

*The circumcision in the temple,* c. 1626
Etching, state II (2), 214 x 160 mm
Bottom left: Rembrandt fecit.
Bottom right: I.P. Berendrech ex
Since 1985 on loan from the
Rijksmuseum, Amsterdam

For the subject of this print see B 47.
This etching, accepted as authentic by
Gersaint in 1751, was subsequently
rejected by Bartsch, Hind and others.
However, it is now generally regarded as
autographic: indeed, it is considered to be
Rembrandt's earliest print. The style is
perhaps still a little clumsy, but it is very
free and vigorous. The print was
published by Berendrecht in Haarlem.

**B 48**

*The circumcision in the temple,* c. 1630
Etching and drypoint
Only state, 88 x 64 mm

For the subject of this print see B 47.

**B 49**
*Simeon's hymn of praise*
*(The presentation in the temple)*, c. 1639
Etching and drypoint
State II (3), 213 x 290 mm

In accordance with the Law of Moses,
Jospeh and Mary presented their
firstborn son in the temple. The old man
Simeon, to whom it had been predicted
that before his death he would see the
Redeemer, recognizes the child and
praises the Lord; the prophetess Anna
also recognizes Christ (Luke 2:22-38).
Into the shadowy space of the temple falls
a ray of light, dramatically illuminating
the chief protagonists: to the right we see
Simeon with the child in his arms and in
the middle the prophetess Anna with the
Holy Ghost in the form of a dove hovering
above her head. The figures in the full
light are indicated principally in outline;
the drypoint has then been used to
elaborate the details to distinguish the
figures from each other.

**B 50**
*The presentation in the temple: in the dark*
*manner*, c. 1654
Etching and drypoint
Only state, 210 x 162 mm

For the subject of this print see B 49.
Simeon, the child in his arms, kneels
before the high priest seated on a dais. In
the middle, towering above the rest, is an
imposing temple guard holding a staff.
On the left, kneeling, are Joseph and
Mary and in the right background we see
a figure probably representing the
prophetess Anna. The whole scene is
shrouded in a mysterious gloom caused by
a close network of lines and hatching
worked up with the drypoint.
Together with prints B 83, 86 and 87 this
etching may be seen as the beginning of a
series about the life of Christ. In
dimensions and technique the sheets are
very similar.

**B 51**
*Simeon's hymn of praise (The presentation in the temple with the angel)*, 1630
Etching, state II (2), 103 x 78 mm
Bottom centre: RHL 1630

For the subject of this print see B 49.

**B 52**
*The flight into Egypt*, 1633
Etching, state I (2), 89 x 62 mm
Bottom centre: Rembrandt inventor et fecit. 1633.

In a dream, an angel warned Joseph that Herod intended to kill the infant Jesus. The same night Joseph and Mary fled into Egypt, taking the child with them (Matthew 2:13-15). The Flight into Egypt was one of Rembrandt's favourite and most frequent subjects.

**B 53**
*The flight into Egypt, by night*, 1651
Etching, burin and drypoint
State VI (6), 127 x 111 mm
Bottom right: Rembrandt f. 1651
(in reverse)
Since 1911 on loan from Teylers Foundation, Haarlem

For the subject of this print see B 52.

**B 55**
*The flight into Egypt: crossing a brook*, 1654
Etching and drypoint
Only state, 93 x 144 mm
Bottom left: Rembrandt f. 1654

This print is one of the series on the youth
of Christ referred to in the commentary to
B 45.

**B 56**
*The flight into Egypt:*
*altered from Segers*, c. 1652
Etching, burin and drypoint
State VI (7), 212 x 284 mm

For the subject of this print see B 52.
Rembrandt was a great admirer of the
work of Hercules Segers (1589/90-c.
1638). He had a number of Segers's rare
paintings in his collection, as well as the
etching plate of Segers's *Tobias and the
angel* (plate 56A). From this he erased the
figures on the right with a scraper,
replacing them (on a much smaller scale)
with Joseph and Mary on their way into
Egypt. He also added the trees in the
background.

plate 56A
Hercules Segers, *Tobias and the angel*,
Amsterdam, Rijksmuseum,
Rijksprentenkabinet.

**B 57**
*The rest on the flight into Egypt,* c. 1644
Etching and drypoint
State III (4), 92 x 59 mm

The Bible says nothing about a rest on the
flight into Egypt. The story became
popular mainly because of the version in
the thirteenth-century collection of tales
about the saints, the *Legenda Aurea*.

**B 58**
*The rest on the flight into Egypt,* 1645
Etching and drypoint
Only state, 130 x 115 mm
Bottom left: Rembrandt f. 1645

For the subject of this print see B 57.
The peaceful and intimate character of
this scene is reinforced by the fact that the
lines have been extremely lightly bitten,
giving the sheet the appearance of a
silverpoint drawing.

**B 60**
*Christ returning from the temple with Joseph
and Mary,* 1654
Etching and drypoint
Only state, 95 x 144 mm
Bottom right: Rembrandt f. 1654

When Jesus was twelve he travelled with
his parents to Jerusalem for the feast of
the Passover. On the way back, Joseph and
Mary suddenly missed him. It turned out
that he had remained in Jerusalem: they
eventually found him in the temple
amongst the doctors of the scriptures. The
three of them then returned home (Luke
2:41-52).
This print is one of the series about the
youth of Christ referred to in the
commentary to B 45.

**B 61**

*Virgin and child in the clouds,* 1641
Etching and drypoint
Only state, 168 x 106 mm
Bottom left: Rembrandt f. 1641

This pre-eminently Catholic theme is rare
in seventeenth-century Dutch art.
Rembrandt took as his model the print of
the same title by the Italian artist Federigo
Barocci (Bartsch 2, plate 61A).
The inverted face level with the
Madonna's left foot is taken by some to be
the reflection of her face in the clouds, but
is regarded by others as an incompletely
erased remnant of an earlier design.

plate 61A
Federigo Barocci, *Virgin and child in the clouds,*
Rotterdam, Museum Boymans-van Beuningen.

**B 62**

*The holy family,* c. 1632
Etching, only state, 96 x 70 mm
Bottom right: RHL

The subject of this print is taken from no particular passage in the Bible. It occurs in Dutch art from the beginning of the fifteenth century. As here, the multitude of familiar domestic details often invests the scene with the character of a genre piece.

**B 63**

*Virgin and child, with the cat and the snake,* 1654
Etching, state I (2), 95 x 145 mm
Bottom centre: Rembrandt. f. 1654.

The unexpected detail of the snake gliding away from under the foot of the Virgin places her in the role of the new Eve, who according to one interpretation of Gen. 3:15 would trample the serpent underfoot. Mary's humility is emphasized by her place on the ground, her holiness by the halo round her head.
This print is one of the series about the youth of Christ referred to in the commentary to B 45.

**B 64**

*Christ disputing with the doctors*, 1654
Etching, only state, 95 x 144 mm
Top left: Rembrandt f. 1654.

In the Bible this scene, in which the twelve-year-old Jesus debates with the teachers of the scriptures in the temple (Luke 2:46-7), precedes the return to Nazareth depicted in B 60. Both prints are part of the series on the youth of Christ referred to in the commentary to B 45. The subject was close to Rembrandt's heart: he also took it for his next two etchings as well as a number of drawings. It gave him an opportunity to use his considerable powers of invention in portraying the scholars' sceptical reactions to the arguments of the self-assured boy.

**B 65**

*Christ disputing with the doctors*, 1652
Etching and drypoint
State I (3), 126 x 214 mm
Bottom left: Rembrandt f. 1652.

For the subject of this print see B 64.

**B 66**

*Christ disputing with the doctors,* 1630
Etching, state III (3), 89 x 68 mm
Bottom centre: RHL 1630

For the subject of this print see B 64.

**B 67**

*Christ preaching (La petite tombe),* c. 1652
Etching, burin and drypoint
Only state, 155 x 207 mm

This scene neither illustrates a specific
passage from the Bible nor has any
iconographical tradition behind it.
The horizontal and vertical lines give the
composition a 'classical' structure - an
indication of the closeness with which
Rembrandt was studying the art of the
Italian Renaissance. A drawing, *Homer
reading his verses* (Benesch 913), which
Rembrandt made in the same year, basing
it on a work by Raphael, is conspicuously
similar to this print.

**B 68**

*The tribute money,* c. 1635
Etching and drypoint
State II (2), 73 x 103 mm

When Christ had driven the moneychangers from the temple (see B 69) the Pharisees, who felt threatened, tried to catch him out with a trick question: was it lawful to give tribute to Caesar? Jesus sent for a coin and asked whose image and superscription appeared on it. When they answered: Caesar's, Jesus said: render therefore unto Caesar the things which are Caesar's and unto God the things that are God's (Matthew 22:15-22).

**B 69**

*Christ chasing the moneychangers from the temple,* 1635
Etching and drypoint
State I (2), 136 x 169 mm
Bottom right: Rembrandt f. 1635

When Jesus entered the temple during the feast of the Passover he found there moneychangers and men buying and selling oxen and sheep. He made a whip of rope and drove these merchants and their beasts out of the temple, overturning the moneychangers' tables (John 2:13-17).

**B 70**

*Christ and the woman from Samaria*, 1658
Etching and drypoint
State III (3), 125 x 160 mm
Left centre: Rembrandt/ f. 1658.

On his way through Samaria Jesus began
talking to a woman at a well. He revealed
himself to her as the Messiah (John 4:5-
42).
In this harmonious composition the
landscape in particular is reminiscent of
Venetian examples.

**B 72**

*The raising of Lazarus*, 1642
Etching, state I (2), 150 x 114 mm
Bottom left: Rembrandt f. 1642.
('2' in reverse)

When Jesus heard that Lazarus, the
brother of Mary and Martha, had died, he
travelled to Bethany, where he
resurrected the dead man. By that time
Lazarus had already been buried four
days (John 11:1-44).

**B 71**

*Christ and the woman from Samaria*, 1634
Etching and drypoint
State I (2), 123 x 106 mm
Top right: Rembrandt f. 1634

For the subject of this print see B 70.

**B 73**
*The raising of Lazarus*, c. 1632
Etching and burin
State VIII (10), 366 x 258 mm

For the subject of this print see B 72.
Some years earlier Rembrandt had
treated this subject in a painting. Many of
the features of this are also found in the
etching.
According to the Bible the miracle took
place in a cave. On the edge of light and
shadow stands Jesus with arm raised. In
the light we see the opened grave from
which Lazarus rises, much to the
astonishment of those standing by.
This is Rembrandt's first monumental
etching. It exists in ten states, showing
how Rembrandt gradually made more
and more changes.

### B 74a

*Christ preaching (The hundred-guilder print),*
c. 1643/49
Etching, drypoint and burin
State II (2), 278 x 388 mm

The subject is a combination of events
described in chapter 19 of St. Matthew's
Gospel, grouped round the figure of
Christ. In the right foreground we see the
sick, coming to be healed (verses 1-2). To
the left are the mothers bringing their
children to see him (verses 13-14) and in
between we see the rich youth who wanted
to have eternal life. Jesus advised him to
sell all his possessions and give the money
to the poor (verses 16-26). The camel in
the gateway on the right probably also
refers to this story: Jesus said that it was
easier for a camel to pass through the eye
of a needle than for a rich man to enter
the kingdom of God (verse 24). In the
background on the left we can see the
Pharisees with whom Jesus entered into a
debate on marriage (verses 3-12).

It is thought that Rembrandt continued to
work on this plate at intervals throughout
the period 1643-49. There are a number
of extant preliminary studies of various
groups and individual figures. In the
sixteenth century this 'hundred-guilder
print' was Rembrandt's most admired
etching. It fetched high prices and after its
first appearance it was soon copied.
The traditional title comes from an early
eighteenth-century story according to
which Rembrandt himself had to pay a
hundred guilders to acquire a copy of the
print.

THE HUNDRED-GUILDER-PRINT.
*Engraved by Rembrandt about the Year 1650 after a few Impressions were printed was laid by & thought to be lost*

**B 74b**
*Christ preaching (The hundred-guilder print),*
printed by William Baillie, c. 1775

When William Baillie bought the etching
plate it was extremely worn. Baillie
somewhat coarsely worked over the entire
plate with the drypoint, issuing an edition
of 100 prints in about 1775. After that the
plate was cut into pieces and loose prints
published from the best parts.
c: the central portion
d: the group of invalids
e: the Pharisees
f: man standing in left foreground

**B 75**
*The agony in the garden,* c. 1657
Etching and drypoint
Only state, 111 x 84 mm

After the Last Supper Jesus went with
three of the disciples to the Mount of
Olives. There, at some distance from
them, he prayed to God to let the cup pass
from him. An angel appeared,
strengthening him. After his prayer he
found that in their sorrow the disciples
had fallen asleep (Luke 22:39-46).

**B 76**

*Christ presented to the people,* 1655
a) Drypoint, state V (8), 358 x 455 mm
b) Drypoint, state VIII (8), 358 x 455 mm
Right centre: Rembrandt f. 1655

After his arrest, Jesus was brought before the Roman governor, Pontius Pilate. Pilate was unconvinced of Jesus' guilt and left the decision as to his execution to the people. Because it was the custom to free a prisoner at the feast of the Passover, he asked the crowd whether he should release Jesus or the murderer Barabbas (Matthew 27:15-26).

a) Here Rembrandt shows us the moment at which Barabbas stands between Jesus and Pilate on the dais, with a crowd gathered in front. Rembrandt has placed the action in an enclosed courtyard in front of a palace of justice with statues of Justice (left) and Fortitude or an Amazon. The composition has been drawn with the drypoint directly onto the plate in free, flowing lines. This was the first time that an etching of so large a format was executed entirely in drypoint. The fragile nature of the burr on the drypoint lines meant that it was constantly necessary to rework the plate. The first states were probably printed in about 1653; after the fifth state Rembrandt started to make drastic changes.

b) Here the crowd in front of the dais has
been removed, concentrating the
spectator's attention on the central group.
In the foreground there are two dark
arches reminiscent of the dungeons under
the city hall so often seen in medieval
paintings.

**B 77**

*Christ before Pilate,* 1636
Etching, state IV (5), 549 x 447 mm
Bottom centre: Rembrandt f. 1636 cum
privile.

Here Rembrandt has followed St. John's
version of the story: Pilate, though not
convinced of Jesus' guilt, had him
scourged. The soldiers then placed a
crown of thorns on Jesus' head, dressed
him in a purple robe and mocked him as
king of the Jews. Pilate then presented
him to the people with the words 'Ecce
Homo' ('Behold the Man'), but finally
gave in to the crowd's wish that Christ be
crucified (John 19:1-16).
For this exceptionally large print
Rembrandt first made, in 1634, a
preliminary study in oils (Bredius 546).
This was executed on paper and indented
onto the plate. It is thought that the
elaboration of the print itself was largely
the work of another artist, possibly J.G.
van Vliet. The chief arguments for this
are the poor quality of the etching and the
fact that in some places whoever was
responsible misinterpreted the
preliminary study (M.R. Kisch, 1984). The
heaviness of the etching, many of the lines
of which have been reinforced with the
burin, indicates that the plate was meant
to be printed in large numbers.
Rembrandt, as the designer, established
his copyright with the inscription 'cum
privile[gio]'.

**B 78**

*The three crosses*, 1653
a) Drypoint and burin
State I (5), 385 x 450 mm
b) Drypoint and burin
State IV (5), 385 x 450 mm
c) Counterproof of state IV
For details of the technique see p. 15.

a) Here Rembrandt shows us the moment of Jesus' death on the cross at Golgotha. A shining light cleaves the darkness that fell over the earth, according to St. Luke (23:33-49), from the sixth until the ninth hour. This light also concentrates all attention on the main protagonists in the drama, as well as introducing a dividing line between Christ's disciples - the 'good' murderer, the traditional group surrounding the fainting Mary, John and the kneeling centurion, who understands the signs and is converted - and the swirling mass of disbelievers in the gloom beyond.

The whole composition was drawn straight into the plate with the drypoint and burin; the figures are set down with swift, sure lines. This impression of the first state has been printed on vellum. This makes the dark passages look even darker than usual because the ink tends to run on the unabsorbent surface.

b) After a number of minor changes Rembrandt signed and dated the third state in 1653. Years later he returned to the plate. Now the drama was reduced even further to essentials. Entire groups of subsidiary figures - in the left foreground, for example - were erased, being replaced by even deeper shadows applied with long, angular scratches with the burin. On the left a new figure has entered the picture: a horseman in Italian Renaissance costume borrowed from a medallion by Pisanello. On the right we can still see St. John, his arms upstretched. Here Rembrandt has gone one step back in time to the moment just before Jesus' death. All these changes have produced a completely new composition in which Christ's suffering is expressed with even more forceful reality.

This print is an early impression of the fourth state, taken from a heavily inked plate so that the details are almost indistinguishable.

c) It is all the more surprising to see how much detail can be discerned in the counterproof of this print.

A counterproof is made by laying a sheet of paper on a newly pulled print, the ink of which is still wet. This new impression is then no longer reversed but parallels the etching plate itself.

**B 79**
*Christ on the cross*, c. 1641
Etching and drypoint
State II (2), 136 x 100 mm

**B 80**
*The small crucifixion*, c. 1635
Etching, only state, 95 x 67 mm
Top centre: Rembrandt f.

**B 81 (II)**
*The descent from the cross*, 1633
Etching and burin
State III or IV (5),
cut to 515 x 400 mm
Bottom centre: Rembrandt f. cum pryvl
°1633

Joseph of Arimathaea, one of the
disciples, obtained permission from Pilate
to remove Jesus' body from the cross; the
corpse was wrapped in linen cloths and
laid in a tomb (John 19:38-40).
The composition is a fairly close copy of
Rembrandt's painting of the same name,
painted for stadtholder Frederick Henry
(Bredius 550). Rembrandt borrowed
elements from Rubens' descent from the
cross of 1611 (Antwerp cathedral), which
he would have known from the print by
Vorsterman. It is possible that the idea of
reproducing one of his own paintings in a
print, and of establishing his sole rights to
the publication ('cum privyl[egio]'), was
also inspired by Rubens. As with B 77, it is
thought that the print is largely the work
of a reproduction engraver, probably J.G.
van Vliet.
The first version of this etching failed in
the acid bath, and only a few impressions
are known.

**B 82**

*The descent from the cross: a sketch,* 1642
Etching and drypoint
Only state, 149 x 116 mm
Bottom right: Rembrandt f. 1642.

For the subject of this print see B 81.

**B 83**

*The descent from the cross by torchlight,* 1654
Etching and drypoint
Only state, 210 x 161 mm
Bottom centre: Rembrandt f. 1654.

For the subject of this print see B 81.
The diagonal structure of the composition
lends greater emphasis to the motion of
removing Christ's body from the cross.
The feeble torchlight against the deep-
black shadows gives a dramatic contrast.
This early impression has been heavily
inked: the drypoint passages come out
very well indeed.
In style and format the print shows many
similarities with B 50, B 86 and B 87; they
may be considered the start of the series.

**B 84**

*Christ carried to the tomb*, c. 1645
Etching and drypoint
Only state, 131 x 108 mm
Bottom centre: Rembrant

After the descent from the cross, Jesus'
body was carried to the tomb that Joseph
of Arimathaea had hewn for himself out
of the rock (Matthew 27:59-60).

**B 86**

*The entombment*, c. 1654
Etching, drypoint and burin
State III (4), 211 x 161 mm
Printed on Japanese paper
Since 1911 on loan from the
Rijksmuseum, Amsterdam

Although the Gospels tell us very little
about the entombment of Christ (see B 84)
it was a popular subject for artists. Often,
as here, we see the grave surrounded by
mourners. They include Joseph of
Arimathaea, Nicodemus and the three
Marys.
This print is one of the series referred to
in the commentary to B 50 and B 83.

**B 87**
*Christ at Emmaus*, 1654
Etching, burin and drypoint
State II (3), 211 x 160 mm
Bottom left: Rembrandt f. 1654.

On Easter Sunday, the third day after his
death (counting the day of his death),
Christ rose from his grave. Unaware of
this resurrection, some of his disciples set
off sadly back for Galilee. On the way
Jesus joined them but they did not
recognize him. It was only when they were
sitting at table in Emmaus and he broke
the bread that their eyes were opened
(Luke 24:13-31). It is this moment of
recognition that Rembrandt shows us
here. This print is one of the series
referred to in the commentary to B 50 and
B 83.

**B 88**
*Christ at Emmaus*, 1634
Etching and drypoint
Only state, 102 x 73 mm
Bottom centre: Rembrandt f. 1634.

For the subject of this print see B 87.

**B 89**

*Christ appearing to the apostles,* 1656
a) Etching, only state, 162 x 210 mm
Bottom centre: Rembrandt f. 1656
b) Counterproof (for a description of
the technique see p. 15)

On the evening of the Resurrection Christ
appeared to his disciples, showing them
his wounds so that they could believe that
he had risen again. The apostle Thomas
refused to believe the story until he had
touched Jesus' wounds for himself. Eight
days later Christ appeared again and
asked Thomas to touch him and believe
(John 20:19-29).

**B 90**

*The good Samaritan,* 1633
Etching and burin
State I (4), 258 x 218 mm
Bottom centre: Rembrandt. inventor et.
Feecit. 1633.

In one of the parables of the New
Testament a Samaritan gives succour to a
man he finds by the wayside who has been
attacked and beaten by robbers. Here
Rembrandt shows us the end of the story:
the two men arriving at an inn. Servants
lift the wounded man from the horse
while the Samaritan pays the innkeeper
(Luke 10:30-5).

**B 91**
*The return of the prodigal son,* 1636
Etching, only state, 156 x 136 mm
Bottom centre: Rembrandt f. 1636
Top centre: 5 *stuyvers*
(in a 17th-century hand)

The subject of this print is again taken
from one of the parables. A man had two
sons, one of whom demanded his
inheritance in advance and left home.
When he returned, having squandered
the lot on loose living, he was nevertheless
joyfully welcomed home by his father
(Luke 15:11-32).
For this monumental composition
Rembrandt borrowed heavily from a
woodcut of the same subject by Maerten
van Heemskerck (Hollstein 53).
According to the inventory of 1656
Rembrandt had copies of numerous
Heemskerck-prints.

**B 92**
*The beheading of John the Baptist,* 1640
Etching and drypoint
State I (2), 129 x 103 mm
Bottom left: Rembrandt f. 1640

John the Baptist, the preacher who
baptized Jesus, was beheaded at the behest
of King Herod. Having pleased him with
her dancing, the king's step-daughter
Salome had asked for John's head on a
platter as a reward (Matthew 14:3-11).

**B 94**

*Peter and John at the gate of the temple*, 1659
Etching, burin and drypoint
State II (4), 180 x 215 mm
Bottom centre: Rembrandt f. 1659
Printed on Japanese paper

Peter and John met a lame beggar before the gates to the temple. Instead of giving him alms, Peter healed him (Acts 3:1-8). Rembrandt situates the scene before the steps of an imposing building representing the second temple: the bronze pillars of the first temple are still intact. This is Rembrandt's last etching of a Biblical subject. The richly tonal chiaroscuro variations produce an almost painterly effect, and in this fine print on Japanese paper full justice is also done to the drypoint passages.

**B 96**

*St. Peter in repentance,* 1645
Etching and drypoint
Only state, 131 x 116 mm
Bottom right: Rembrandt f. 1645.

As soon as the cock crowed, Peter realized
that he had three times denied Jesus as he
had foretold (Matthew 26:75).
The figure of Peter, identified by his
attribute, the keys, has been etched very
lightly, so that the print looks almost like a
silverpoint drawing.

**B 97**

*The stoning of St. Stephen,* 1635
Etching, state I (2), 95 x 85 mm
Bottom left: Rembrandt f. 1635.

St. Stephen was summoned before the
court at the instigation of jealous priests.
When he had a vision in which Christ
appeared to him at the side of God he was
driven out of the city and stoned, thus
becoming the first Christian martyr (Acts
7:54-60).
Rembrandt had already depicted this
subject in a painting (Bredius 531A) from
which many of the details in this print are
taken.

**B 98**

*The baptism of the eunuch,* 1641
Etching, state II (2), 178 x 213 mm
Bottom right: Rembrandt/ f. 1641

Philip the Evangelist had been charged by
an angel to take the road from Jerusalem
to Gaza. There he met a eunuch, a
dignitary of the Ethiopian court. Philip
converted him and baptized him in a body
of water they happened to be passing
(Acts 8:26-39).

**B 99**

*The death of the Virgin*, 1639
Etching and drypoint
State II (3), 409 x 315 mm
Bottom left: Rembrandt f. 1639

The account of the death of the Virgin
does not appear in the New Testament,
only in the apocryphal literature.
For his large, baroque composition
Rembrandt has borrowed a number of
elements from Dürer's woodcuts of the
birth and death of the Virgin (Bartsch 80
and 93).

**B 101**

*St. Jerome praying,* 1632
Etching, state I (3), 109 x 81 mm
Bottom right: Rembrandt ft. 1632
Since 1948 on loan from a private
collection

St. Jerome - scholar, translator of the
Bible and one of the four original Doctors
(teachers) of the Church - is often
depicted by artists as a hermit. He is
almost always accompanied by the lion
which according to legend remained
faithful to him after he had removed a
thorn from its paw.
Rembrandt devoted seven etchings and a
number of drawings to this Catholic saint.
In fact he quite often chose Catholic
subjects (e.g. B 99 and B 107); he was
evidently not particularly dogmatic in his
views.

**B 102**

*St. Jerome kneeling in prayer,* 1635
Etching, only state, 114 x 80 mm
Top right: Rembrandt/ f. 1635

For the subject of this print see B 101.

**B 103**

*St. Jerome beside a pollard willow,* 1648
Etching and drypoint
State II (2), 180 x 133 mm
Bottom left: Rembrandt f. 1648

For the subject of this print see B 101.
The scene is dominated by a study of a
pollarded willow, elaborately detailed with
the drypoint. However, instead of the
meadows that one might expect to see
behind such a tree we find, drawn quite
loosely and casually, St. Jerome at his
writing-table. Decaying trees are quite a
common iconographical feature in scenes
of St. Jerome.
In this exceptionally fine impression the
drypoint work has not yet lost anything of
its power.

**B 104**

*St. Jerome reading in an Italian landscape,*
c. 1654
Etching, burin and drypoint
State I (2), 259 x 210 mm
Printed on Japanese paper

For the subject of this print see B 101.
St. Jerome, engrossed in his book, sits in a
hilly landscape. The buildings on the top
of the hill, intended to represent Jerome's
monastery near Bethlehem, remind one
more of Italy than anywhere else. This
landscape and the harmonious
composition are unquestionably borrowed
from the work of Venetian artists. This
impression is reinforced by the sunny
atmosphere evoked by the golden-yellow
Japanese paper. In his collection
Rembrandt had two books of prints after
Titian, so he must have been familiar with
landscapes like this (see also B 107).

**B 105**
*St. Jerome in a dark chambre,* 1642
Etching, burin and drypoint
State II (2), 151 x 173 mm
Bottom centre: Rembrandt f. 1642.
Heavily inked impression

For the subject of this print see B 101.

**B 107**
*St. Francis beneath a tree praying,* 1657
Drypoint and etching
State II (2), 180 x 244 mm
Bottom right: Rembrandt f. 1657.
Printed with surface tone on Japanese
paper
Since 1911 on loan
from the Rijksmuseum, Amsterdam

In 1224 the mystic and ecclesiastical
reformer St. Francis of Assisi and another
monk went into retreat in a remote part of
Tuscany. While praying to God he
received there the stigmata (the wounds
suffered by Christ on the Cross).
Rembrandt shows us not the moment
most commonly depicted, at which Francis
receives the stigmata, but the prayer that
preceded that event.
As the incomplete first state of the print
shows, the order in which the artist went
to work was the reverse of his usual
practice. First he drew - with the drypoint
only - the major part of the foreground; in
the second state the hut behind the saint
and the landscape on the right were
etched in.

# *Allegorical scenes*

Allegorical scenes are intended to be taken figuratively rather than literally. They express abstract concepts or events through the medium of particular images - perhaps a figure with a special attribute or symbol - from which the informed spectator can deduce the meaning.

**B 109**

*Death appearing to a wedded couple*, 1639
Etching, only state, 109 x 79 mm
Bottom left: Rembrandt./ f. 1639

Death, in the shape of a skeleton carrying an hour-glass (the symbol of Time), rises from a grave before a young couple who are seen in elegant sixteenth-century costume. The scene may be interpreted as an illustration of the transience of life.

**B 110**

*The Phoenix or the statue overthrown*, 1658
Etching and drypoint
Only state, 179 x 183 mm
Bottom right: Rembrandt f. 1658.
Printed on Japanese paper

The bird on the pedestal, flanked by trumpeting angels, is Phoenix rising from the ashes, a symbol of resurrection. The figure lying on its back in the foreground presumably represents Envy: the serpent wound round its arm would appear to point in that direction. The meaning of this scene is unclear, but several writers have seen it as some kind of political commentary.

The print is a particularly fine impression on light Japanese paper in which the drypoint passages come out well.

# *Book illustrations*

**B 111**

*The ship of fortune*, 1633
Etching, state II (2), 113 x 166 mm
Right centre, on the ship: Rembrandt f.
1633. (partially scraped away)

This etching appears at the beginning of
Elias Herckmans's 'Der Zee-Vaert Lof' of
1634, which begins with a description of
the emperor Augustus's victory over Mark
Antony in the naval battle of Actium in 31
BC. As a sign of peace the gates of the
temple of Janus are symbolically closed.
The temple is in the left background.
Janus himself, a Roman god, is
traditionally depicted as a bust with two
faces looking in opposite directions. In the
left foreground, seated on the fallen
charger, we see the emperor Augustus
wearing a laurer wreath.
Elsewhere in his book Herckmans
explains that the coming of peace will lead
to a new flourishing of sea-trade. This is

represented symbolically by the small ship
seen putting to sea. The female figure
hoisting the sail is probably Bellona, the
goddness of war and sister of Mars, god of
war, perhaps the man sitting at the stern.
With the declaration of peace they can
now leave the battlefield. Some authors
regard the female figure as the goddness
Fortune.

**B 112a**

*Medea: or the marriage of Jason and Creusa,*
1648
Etching and drypoint
State IV (5), 240 x 176 mm
Bottom right: Rembrandt. f. 1648

Jason abandoned his wife Medea to marry
Creusa. To exact her revenge, Medea sent
Creusa a wedding gift consisting of a
mantle soaked in poison. At bottom right
we see Medea with the gifts and a dagger.
The etching served as an illustration for
the printed edition of Jan Six's tragedy
'Medea', which was published in 1648
following performance a year earlier.

**B 112b** (not reproduced)
Jan Six
*Medea*, Amsterdam 1648

A copy of the first edition of Jan Six's
tragedy 'Medea', with the fourth state of
Rembrandt's etching. In the book the
plate has been better printed and there is
a greater light/dark contrast than in the
loose etching.

**B 113**
See p. 92

# Hunting scenes

**B 114**

*The large lion hunt,* 1641
Etching and drypoint
State II (2), 224 x 300 mm
Top right: Rembrandt f./ 1641

This etching, like the next two, is based
partly on several engravings of hunting
scenes made by the sixteenth-century
Italian artist Antonio Tempesta (Bartsch
1138, 1139, 1148). From the inventory of
1656 we know that Rembrandt possessed
four volumes of prints by Tempesta. One
striking feature of this particular etching
is the sketch-like drypoint passages, which
are reminiscent of Rembrandt's earlier
treatment of the subject in 1629-30 (B 115
and B 116).

**B 115**
*The small lion hunt (with two lions)*, c. 1629
Etching, only state, 154 x 121 mm

The rough-and-ready execution suggests
a date between 1629 and 1630.

**B 116**
*The small lion hunt (with one lion)*, c. 1629
Etching only state, 158 x 117 mm

# Genre scenes

The term 'genre scene' is used here in a general sence to refer to a number of prints covering a wide range of subjects: street scenes, beggars, peasant scenes, drinking scenes, domestic interiors, and so on.

In the strict sense in which the term is used today, genre scenes are those that give us the impression of having been drawn from everyday life, though in reality they were composed in the studio. In this sense, genre scenes were never spontaneous records of actual events. Rather, they show us a construct used by the artists of the seventeenth century to convey an idea, issue an admonition or deliver a sermon (E. de Jongh, 1976). Those by Adriaen Brouwer and Adriaen van Ostade are a case in point. Rembrandt's genre scenes generally offer too little by way of allusion for us to be able to attach any particular moralizing content to them. Even so, some of them may have a deeper meaning than appears at first sight.

**B 117**
*A cavalry fight*, c. 1632
Etching, state II (2), 103 x 78 mm

**B 113**
*The star of the Kings: a night piece*, c. 1651
Etching with touches of drypoint
Only state, 94 x 143 mm

This is the feast of Epiphany or the Three Kings, as celebrated by Dutch children: going round the houses with a lighted lantern in the shape of a star.

**B 118**

*Three Oriental figures (Jacob and Laban?),*
1641
Etching, state II (2), 145 x 114 mm
Top right: Rembrandt f. 1641 (in reverse)

The scene depicted here may be the
argument between Jacob and Laban:
Jacob wished to return to Canaan with his
wives Leah and Rachel and his children,
but his father-in-law Laban tried to
dissuade him (Gen. 30:25-34).

**B 119**

*The strolling musicians,* c. 1635
Etching, state I (2), 138 x 115 mm

An old man with a barrel organ and a
young man with bagpipes play before a
married couple standing with their child
in the doorway of their house.

**B 120**

*The Spanish gipsy Preciosa*, c. 1642
Etching, only state, 133 x 113 mm

This print probably illustrates a scene
from Cervantes' play 'Preciosa'. It tells the
story of Preciosa, who as a child is
abducted by the old gypsy woman
Majombe to be taught by her the wisdom
of the gypsies. The piece ends with the
marriage of Preciosa to a Spanish
nobleman. Several Dutch versions of the
play appeared and were performed in
about 1643.

**B 121**

*The rat-poison pedlar (The rat catcher)*, 1632
Etching, state III (3), 140 x 125 mm
Bottom right: RHL 1632
(the last two numerals are reversed)

On the end of a pole the pedlar carries a
basket containing live rats; dead animals
hang below it as proof of the efficacy of
the poison being peddled.
This print was extremely popular in the
sixteenth century. Many impressions of it
are known and it was also frequently
copied.

**B 123**

*The goldsmith*, 1655
Etching and drypoint
State I (2), 77 x 56 mm
Bottom left: Rembrandt f. 1655
Printed on Japanese paper

Here we see the goldsmith putting the final touches to a figure of Caritas, the personification of charity.

**B 124**

*The pancake woman*, 1635
Etching, state II (3), 109 x 77 mm
Bottom centre: Rembrandt. ft 1635

For his version of this popular subject Rembrandt probably drew inspiration from a work by Adriaan Brouwer. The inventory of 1656 refers to a painting by Brouwer of a similar subject.

**B 125**

*The golf player*, 1654
Etching, state I (2), 95 x 143 mm
Bottom left: Rembrandt f. 1654.

**B 126**
*Jews in the synagogue*, 1648
Etching and drypoint
State II (3), 71 x 129 mm
Top centre: Rembrandt. f./ 1648.

The subject of this print is unclear. In the inventory of the collection of Clement de Jonghe of 1679 the plate is called 'Pharisees in the temple', suggesting that it is a Biblical scene. However, in the inventory of the collection of Valerius Röver of 1731 it is referred to as 'The temple of Jews', while Gersaint (1751) speaks of 'Synagogue des Juifs'. In any event, Rembrandt must have etched the scene from his imagination since there was no large synagogue in Amsterdam before 1670.

**B 128**
*Woman at a door hatch talking to a man and children*, 1641
Etching, only state, 93 x 61 mm
Top centre: Rembrandt/ f. 1641

**B 129**
*The quacksalver*, 1635
Etching, only state, 78 x 36 mm
Bottom centre: Rembrandt. ft 1635

**B 130**
*Man drawing from a cast*, c. 1641
Etching, state II (3), 94 x 64 mm

This print probably illustrates the view, commonly subscribed to in the seventeenth century, that an artist or aspiring artist could only achieve the highest perfectionism in art by constant practice.

**B 131**
*Peasant family on the tramp*, c. 1632
Etching, state II (2), 113 x 93 mm

**B 133**
*A peasant in a high cap, leaning on a stick*, 1639
a) Etching, only state, 83 x 45 mm
Bottom centre: Rembrandt. f 1639
b) idem
Printed by Beaumont in 1906

**B 135**
*Peasant with his hands behind his back,* 1631
Etching and burin
State I (4), 59 x 48 mm
Top left: RHL 1631 (possibly by another hand)

**B 136**
*The card player,* 1641
Etching, state I (3), 88 x 82 mm
Left centre: Rembrandt f/ 1641

**B 138**
*The blind fiddler,* 1631
Etching, state III (3), 78 x 53 mm
Bottom centre: RHL 1631

**B 139**
*Turbaned soldier on a horse,* c. 1632
Etching, only state, 82 x 57 mm
Top right: RHL (in reverse)

**B 140**
*Man with a hurdy-gurdy*, c. 1631
Etching, only state, 82 x 57 mm
Early impression

**B 148**
*Student at a table by candlelight*, c. 1642
Etching, only state, 147 x 133 mm
Bottom right: Rembrandt

The very dark passages in the etching are
the result of a fine veil of cross-hatching.
The only light source is the flickering
flame of the oil lamp.

**B 143**
*Old man seen from behind*, c. 1631
a) Etching, state II (4), 72 x 42 mm
b) Etching, state IV (4), 72 x 42 mm

This study was originally part of a larger
plate with several etched heads of old men
which was subsequently cut into five
pieces. In the fourth state it was reworked
by another artist, probably J.G. van Vliet.

**B 150**
*Beggar with his left hand extended,* 1631
Etching, state IV (4), 63 x 41 mm
Top left: RHL 1631

Probably only the first state of this print
was executed by Rembrandt. All the later
states are thought to have been reworked
by J.G. van Vliet.

**B 151**
*Man in a coat and fur cap, leaning against a
bank,* c. 1630
Etching, state III (3), 112 x 79 mm
Top right: RHL (in reverse)

**B 152**
*The Persian,* 1632
Etching, only state, 108 x 79 mm
Bottom centre: RHL 1632
(the last two numerals are reversed)

This etching owes its traditional title, *The
Persian,* to the finely detailed and exotic
costume worn by the model.

**B 156**
*The skater,* c. 1639
Etching and drypoint
Only state, 61 x 59 mm

**B 157**
*The hog*, 1643
Etching and drypoint
State I (2), 145 x 184 mm
Bottom right: Rembrandt. f/ 1643.

The small boy behind the sow holds an
inflated pig's bladder and a straw. This
may hint at a hidden meaning: like
blowing soap-bubbles, in the seventeenth
century blowing up a pig's bladder was a
familar symbol of transience.
In contrast to the rather sketchily drawn
figures in the background, the sow, legs
bound ready for the slaughter, has been
worked up in detail.

**B 158**
*Sleeping puppy*, c. 1640
Etching and drypoint
State III (3), 39 x 81 mm

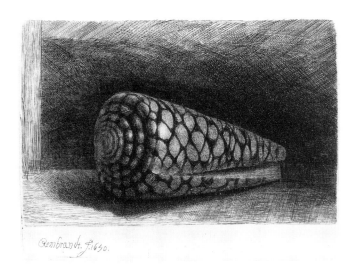

**B 159**
*The shell (Conus Marmoreus)*, 1650
Etching, drypoint and burin
State II (3), 97 x 132 mm
Bottom left: Rembrandt. f. 1650.

The shell seen here was almost certainly
part of the collection of shells in
Rembrandt's 'art room', referred to in the
inventory of 1656. It is the only still life
that Rembrandt ever etched.

**B 162**
*Beggar in a high cap, leaning on a stick,*
c. 1629
Etching, only state, 156 x 120 mm

**B 163**
*Beggar leaning on a stick, facing left,* c. 1630
Etching, only state, 85 x 46 mm

### Beggars and
### street figures

In the years around 1630 Rembrandt
made a large number of studies of beggars
and other street characters. Unlike his
predecessors and contemporaries, in his
depictions of these people Rembrandt did
not stress their often horrifying physical
deformities or their distressed
circumstances; nor is there the slightest
sign of any amusement at their
misfortunes. Instead, he shows us these
outcasts in a manner imbued with human
understanding.

In the earliest sheets, which go back to the
Leiden period, the beggars are depicted in
a swiftly executed, sketchy way
reminiscent of Jacques Callot, whose
beggar series of 1622 seems to have been
one of Rembrandt's sources of inspiration.
Then, in about 1630, Rembrandt begins
to pay more attention to the contrast
between light and dark, at the same time
taking more care over the details. He
returned to the general theme in the
second half of the 1640s.

**B 164**
*Beggar man and beggar woman conversing,*
*1630*
Etching, only state, 78 x 66 mm
Bottom left: RHL 1630
(the '3' was originally a '2')

**B 170**
*Beggar woman leaning on a stick,* 1646
Etching and drypoint
Only state, 82 x 63 mm
Bottom left: Rembrandt. f 1646

**B 168**
*Old beggar woman with a gourd,* c. 1629
Etching, state II (2), 103 x 46 mm

**B 173**
*Beggar seated, warming his hands at a brazier,*
c. 1630
Etching, state II (2), 77 x 46 mm

The man warms his hands at an
earthenware pot filled with glowing coals.

**B 172**
*Ragged peasant with his hands behind him,*
*holding a stick,* c. 1630
Etching, state V (6), 92 x 67 mm

**B 174**

*Beggar seated on a bank,* 1630
Etching, only state, 116 x 70 mm
Bottom centre: RHL 1630

The beggar in this etching is very
probably a self-portrait of Rembrandt.
The facial expression resembles that in
some of the small self-portrait studies such
as B 13 (plate 174A).

plate 174A
Rembrandt, *Self-portrait*
Amsterdam, Rijksmuseum,
Rijksprentenkabinet.

**B 176**

*Beggars receiving alms at the door of a house,*
1648
Etching, drypoint and burin
State I (3), 165 x 128 mm
Bottom right: Rembrandt. f. 1648.

It is interesting to compare this print with
a much earlier one of similar composition,
*The rat-poison pedlar* (B 121). The print of
the beggars at the door shows how far
Rembrandt has progressed in the
intervening sixteen years. Here the whole
structure of the picture is simpler and
more readily appreciated: details that
distract the attention have disappeared
and the result is less picturesque, but there
is greater strength in the way the forms
are conveyed.

**B 177**

*A peasant calling out: 'tis vinnich kout' (it's damned cold)*, 1634
Etching, only state, 112 x 39 mm
Top right: Rembrandt/ f. 1634
Top centre: *tis vinnich kout*

This etching and the following one (B 178) belong together, illustrating how two peasants discuss the weather. Two small prints by the German artist Hans Sebald Beham from 1542 (Bartsch 188 and 189), in which the same conversation takes place, served Rembrandt as models. The amusing thing about these two etchings is that here the two peasants are standing back to back, whereas in the original version by Beham they face one another.

**B 178**

*A peasant, replying: 'dats niet' (that's not)*, 1634
Etching, only state, 112 x 39 mm
Top right: Rembran/ f 163
(the last numeral, a '4', is missing)
Top centre: *dats niet*

For commentary see B 177.

**Bartsch 188**
**Hans Sebald Beham**
*'Es ist kalt Weter'*
Woodcut, 45 x 30 mm
Right centre: HSB; top left:
15; top right: 42

**Bartsch 189**
**Hans Sebald Beham**
*'Das schadet nit'*
Woodcut, 45 x 30 mm
Left centre: HSB

**B 179**
*Beggar with a wooden leg,* c. 1630
Etching, state I (2), 114 x 66 mm

In the inventory of Clement de Jonghe of
1679 this print appears under the title
'Capteijn eenbeen' (Captain One-leg) -
probably the name given to some well-
known figure of the Amsterdam streets.

**B 188**
*The flute player (Owlglass),* 1642
Etching and drypoint
State III (4), 116 x 143 mm
Bottom centre: Rembrandt. f/ 1642
('2' reversed)

At first sight this appears to be a rural
idyll, but there are a number of elements
that appear to imbue it with a negative
and erotic undertone. The owl is the
symbol of the night, for example, and the
goat a symbol of lust. Since the eighteenth
century, however, this print has been
known as *Tijl Uylenspiegel* or *Owlglass.*
After this state Rembrandt removed the
face of the figure in the background,
whose role is obscure.

**B 189**
*The sleeping herdsman*, c. 1644
Etching and burin
Only state, 78 x 57 mm

**B 190**
*A man making water*, 1631
Etching, only state, 82 x 48 mm
Bottom centre: RHL 1631

This print has a pendant in the *Woman making water* (B 191, plate 190A).

plate 190A
Rembrandt, *A woman making water*,
Haarlem, Teylers Museum.

# Studies of nudes

In a number of drawings by Rembrandt and his pupils the same model is seen from different angles. From this we may legitimately conclude that in Rembrandt's studio nudes and other models were drawn from life. The etched male nudes of about 1646 (B 193, B 194 and B 196) were presumably also made from life. The attitudes of the models seem to confirm this: these are truly academic poses like those found in seventeenth-century books of examples for student artists.

Between 1658 and 1661 Rembrandt made a series of etchings of female nudes. Here the loose, open drawing style of the male nudes of the mid 1640s has been abandoned. Instead, Rembrandt uses all the possibilities of light and dark: it is this, rather than any actual outline, that gives the shapes their volume.

Rembrandt often depicts his models extremely realistically, even in his early work: witness B 198. This extreme realism did not accord with the notion of beauty that was current in his day and it was accordingly not always greeted with enthusiasm by his contemporaries. Wenzel Hollar, on the other hand, copied Rembrandt's realistic nude of *c.*1631 (B 198) as early as 1635.

**B 192**
*Artist drawing from a model,* c. 1639
Etching, drypoint and burin
State II (2), 232 x 184 mm

Seated amidst the usual paraphernalia of the studio - weapons, plaster cast, easel and canvas - we see an artist drawing a female nude from life. The model stands on a small platform holding a palm frond. The print is presumably intended as a glorification of the draughtsman's art: as would seem to be confirmed by the palm frond and studio props. The work was never finished: only the dark background is completely worked, the foreground remaining little more than an outline sketch.

**B 193**

*Seated male nude,* 1646
Etching, state I (2), 164 x 96 mm
Bottom left: Rembrandt f. 1646.

The model sits on a stool placed on a
platform so that everyone in the studio
can see him properly. A drawing by one of
Rembrandt's pupils (Benesch A 48, plate
193A) shows the same model in the same
pose but from a different angle. Clearly,
Rembrandt drew his etching direct onto
the plate, while his pupils were drawing
the same model. In the etching, of course,
the method of printing has reversed the
image.

plate 193A
Rembrandt-pupil, *Seated male nude,*
Paris, Bibliotèque Nationale.

**B 195**
*The bathers*, 1651
Etching, state I (2), 110 x 137 mm
Bottom left: Rembrandt. f 1651
(the '5' has been changed from a '3'
with the drypoint)
Printed with light tone on Japanese paper

**B 194**
*Male nude seated and standing (The walking
frame)*, c. 1646
Etching, state II (3), 194 x 128 mm

In the foreground we see two studies of
the same young man: standing and sitting.
In the background, very lightly etched, we
see a woman teaching a child to walk with
the aid of a baby walker.
This print should be seen as a
metaphorical exhortation to 'keep trying':
the child must learn to walk and the artist
must practise constantly to master his art.

**B 196**
*Seated male nude, one leg extended*, 1646
Etching, state II (2), 97 x 168 mm
Bottom left: Rembrandt. f. 1646.

In subject and style this print is closely
related to B 193. Here again the model is
probably posing for both Rembrandt and
his pupils.

**B 197**
*Woman sitting half dressed beside a stove*, 1658
Etching, drypoint and burin
State III (7), 228 x 187 mm
Top right: Rembrandt f. 1658.

The half-dressed woman sits beside a
stove decorated with a relief of Mary
Magdalene kneeling before a crucifix.

**B 198**
*Naked woman seated on a mound*, c. 1631
Etching, state I (2), 177 x 160 mm
Top left: RHL

**B 199**
*Woman at the bath with a hat beside her*, 1658
Etching and drypoint
State II (2), 156 x 129 mm
Top left: Rembrandt. f. 1658.

**B 200**
*Naked woman, bathing her feet at a brook*,
1658
Etching, only state, 160 x 80 mm
Top left: Rembrandt./ f. 1658.
Printed on very thin and white paper

Despite the tree-trunk and the foliage in
the background, this nude study has every
appearance of having been done in the
studio: the model is seated on a large
cushion and behind her there is what
looks very much like the back of a chair.

**B 201**
*Diana bathing*, c. 1631
Etching, only state, 178 x 159 mm
Bottom right: RHL. f.

This print derives its title from the quiver
seen at the left. Bow and arrow are the
attributes of Diana, the mythical goddess
of hunting. Still, it is principally a study of
the female nude. The composition was
first drawn on paper in black chalk
(Benesch 21) and then transferred onto
the etching plate.

**B 202**
*Woman with an arrow (Cleopatra?)*, 1661
Etching, drypoint and burin
State II (3), 205 x 123 mm
Bottom left: Rembrndt. f. 1661.
(the 'd' is reversed)
Printed with surface tone

To the left, behind the nude woman, we
see the face of a young man. The meaning
of this scene is obscure. The classical
appearance of the woman's hair may
indicate a mythical subject and the scene
has been interpreted as Venus arming
Cupid with the arrow, his attribute. On
the other hand she may be mocking him,
having succeeded in tricking him out of
the arrow. Others believe the two figures
to be Antony and Cleopatra. It has also
been suggested that the woman is not
holding an arrow at all, but rather keeping
the curtains of the bed together.

**B 203**
*Jupiter and Antiope*, 1659
Etching, drypoint and burin
State I (2), 138 x 205 mm
Bottom centre: Rembrandt/ f. 1659
Printed on Japanese paper

This print illustrates the mythological
story of Jupiter, having assumed the form
of a satyr, visiting Antiope, daughter of
the king of Thebes, as she sleeps. In
composition the print is based on an
etching by Annibale Carracci (Bartsch 17,
plate 203A).

plate 203A
Annibale Carracci, *Jupiter and Antiope*,
Amsterdam, Rijksmuseum,
Rijksprentenkabinet.

**B 204**
*Jupiter and Antiope*, c. 1631
Etching, state II (2), 84 x 114 mm
Right centre: RHL

The subject is the same as that of B 203,
*Jupiter and Antiope*. This etching was made
28 years before the second version and
lacks the subtle play of light and dark that
was later to characterize Rembrandt's
etching technique.

**B 205**
*Negress lying down*, 1659
Etching, drypoint and burin
State II (3), 81 x 158 mm
Bottom left: Rembrandt/ f. 1658.

# *Landscapes*

Rembrandt's landscape etchings were all produced between 1640 and 1653. In 1639 he had bought his house on the Breestraat (the present museum). From here he could quickly be outside the city, walking east along the St. Anthoniesdijk to Diemen or south along the Amstel to Ouderkerk. Many of the subjects of his landscape etchings can be localized to one of these routes.

These landscape etchings can be divided into two groups: those executed between 1640 and 1645 and those made in 1650-53. The first group consists of pure etchings, often with a carefully elaborated foreground motif against a lightly indicated horizon. In the second group the etched ground is worked up with the drypoint and burin. At the same time the characteristic Dutch landscapes of many of the works in this second group have additional fantasy elements such as mountains and exotic buildings.

**B 207**
*Small grey landscape,* c. 1640
Etching, only state, 38 x 82 mm

Rembrandt's first landscape etching is a tiny dusk scene of a house by a tree-lined body of water. Only the changes in direction and spacing of the hatching enable us to discern the individual elements of the composition.

**B 208**

*Six's bridge,* 1645
Etching, state II (3), 129 x 224 mm
Bottom right: Rembrandt f. 1645
Inscribed in an 18th-century hand:
*mijn Heer Six en Brugh*

The traditional title, to which the
inscription in an eighteenth-century hand
also refers, is inaccurate. The scene is *not*
the country estate of Jan Six (which was in
Hillegom) but more probably that which
belonged to the Amsterdam burgomaster
Albert Burgh, which was on the Amstel.
To the left of the picture we see the
steeple of Ouderkerk church, a good
fifteen miles away from Hillegom. This is
one of Rembrandt's most spontaneous,
drawing-like landscape etchings. It gives
the distinct impression of having been
made in the open air.

**B 209**

*The Omval,* 1645
Etching and drypoint
State II (2), 184 x 225 mm
Bottom right: Rembrant 1645

Rembrandt drew the piece of land in the
bend of the Amstel, still called the Omval
today, several times. Here we look over
the river to the houses, windmills and
boats at the entrance to the canal
encircling the Diemermeer. In the left
foreground there is a finely wrought
decaying pollarded willow, in the shadows
of which two lovers sit; the young man is
placing a wreath of flowers on his
beloved's head.
This is the first of Rembrandt's landscape
etchings in which he makes extensive use
of drypoint, particularly noticeable in the
tree.

**B 210**

*View of Amsterdam,* c. 1640
Etching, only state, 112 x 153 mm

Here Rembrandt has drawn the city from
the north-east, sitting on the Kadijk and
looking over the meadows and the Y with
its ships and boats. The silhouette of the
city is carefully drawn, though it is
naturally reversed by the printing process.
From left to right we see the
Haringpakkerstoren, the Oude Kerk, the
Montelbaanstoren, the warehouses of the
Dutch East India Company, the windmill
on the Rijzenhoofd, the Zuiderkerk, and
the windmills along the eastern walls of
the city as far as the Blauwbrug. Because
of the low viewpoint the darkly detailed
foreground becomes more prominent in
the scene and the skyline of the city stands
in sharp contrast to the horizon.

**B 211**
*Landscape with shepherd and dog*, c. 1653
Etching and drypoint
State II (2), 129 x 157 mm

This is probably the last of Rembrandt's
landscape etchings. The typically Dutch
foreground is bounded by an imaginary
mountain landscape with exotic buildings.

**B 212**

*The three trees,* 1643
Etching, drypoint and burin
Only state, 213 x 279 mm
Bottom left: Rembrandt f. 1643

This louring sky is most unusual for Rembrandt's etched landscapes. The thunder-clouds and the false sunlight produce a dramatic contrast. From the dike with its three large trees a flat expanse stretches away into the distance, populated by numerous tiny figures. The silhouette on the horizon appears to be that of Amsterdam. Though topographically not very accurate, the view was probably drawn from a point somewhere on the Haarlemmerdijk to the west of the city (C. Campbell, 1980).

**B 213**

*Landscape with a fisherman*, c. 1652
Etching and drypoint
State II (2), 66 x 174 mm

This farm on the St. Anthoniesdijk also
appears in another etching, B 224, though
there it is seen from a different angle. To
Rembrandt and his pupils it was a popular
motif and it recurs in several prints and
drawings. From the crown of the dike we
see the Y crowded with shipping. The
unexpected mountains in the background
were only added in the second state.

**B 217**

*Three gabled cottages beside a road*, 1650
Etching and drypoint
State III (3),l 161 x 202 mm
Bottom left: Rembrandt f. 1650

The road passing by the farm cottages
runs diagonally through the picture,
creating a highly effective impression of
depth. These cottages with their pointed
gables are characteristic of the countryside
near Amsterdam but nothing is known of
their exact location. In this etching
Rembrandt has made extensive use of the
drypoint, seen most notably in the trees.

**B 218**
*Landscape with a square tower,* 1650
Etching and drypoint
State IV (4), 88 x 156 mm
Bottom right: Rembrandt f./ 1650

**B 219**
*Landscape with a man sketching,* c. 1645
Etching, only state, 129 x 209 mm

**B 220**

*The shepherd and his family*, 1644
Etching and drypoint
Only state, 95 x 67 mm
Top left: Rembrandt/ f. 1644

**B 222**

*Clump of trees with a vista*, 1652
Drypoint, state II (2), 124 x 211 mm
Bottom right: Rembrandt f 1652.
Since 1911 on loan from the
Rijksmuseum, Amsterdam

Rembrandt drew this group of trees
several times. They probably stood beside
the Amstel. The entire print has been
made with the drypoint, i.e. by scratching
straight into the copper plate, in a most
spontaneous, freehand manner.

**B 223**
*Farms and tower surrounded by trees*, c. 1651
Etching and drypoint
State IV (4), 123 x 318 mm

The house amongst the trees is probably
'Het Torentje', a country estate on the
road to Amstelveen that belonged to Jan
Uytenboogaert (see B 281). This is one of
the few prints to feature a cloudy sky. The
plate has been printed with surface tone,
i.e. a certain amount of ink has been left
on the flat areas. This gives the effect of a
grey wash over the whole print.

**B 224**
*Landscape with a flock of sheep*, 1652
Etching and drypoint
State II (2), 82 x 172 mm
Bottom left: Rembrandt f 1652
('d' in reverse)

For commentary see B 213.

B 225
*Cottage with a haybarn*, 1641
Etching and drypoint
Only state, 129 x 321 mm
Bottom right: Rembrandt f/ 1641

There are various recognizable motifs in
this print which Rembrandt probably
sketched from life, later putting them
together to make a fantasized but entirely
typical landscape. On the right are the
ruins of Kostverloren House and to the
left a skyline reminiscent of that of
Amsterdam.

**B 226**
*Cottage and a large tree*, 1642
Etching, only state, 127 x 320 mm
Bottom right: Rembrandt f/ 1642

**B 227**
*Landscape with an obelisk*, c. 1650
Etching and drypoint
State II (2), 83 x 160 mm

The 'obelisk' of the title is the 'banishing post' at Spieringerhorn, near Halfweg between Amsterdam and Haarlem. Such boundary posts marked the limits of the city's jurisdiction. In the second state the obelisk was lengthened to extend beyond the scene: traces of the original top can still be seen.

**B 228**
*Farmhouses beside a canal*, c. 1645
Etching, only state, 140 x 207 mm

This is probably a view of Ouderkerk. With the low horizon most of the picture is taken up by sky. The atmospheric effect is heightened by printing the sheet with surface tone.

**B 232**
*Cottage with a white paling,* 1648
Etching and drypoint
State II (3), 130 x 158 mm
Bottom left: Rembrandt f

This is one of the rare landscape etchings
that Rembrandt based on drawings
(Benesch C 41, plate 232A). The etching
has a number of typical details of rural life
not seen in the drawing and the cottage is
now set in a wider landscape.

plate 232A
Rembrandt, *Cottage with a wooden paling,*
Amsterdam, Rijksmuseum,
Rijksprentenkabinet.

## B 233
*The windmill,* 1641

a) Etching, only state, 145 x 208 mm
Bottom right: Rembrandt f 1641
Early impression

b) Etching, only state, 145 x 208 mm
Bottom right: Rembrandt f 1641
Inscribed on the back in 17th-century handwriting: *den Wijntmolen van den pester van/Ossenbruggen en heft hem geervet van/ sijn beste vader*

Lugt has demonstrated that this is one of the windmills on the fortifications round Amsterdam, in this case the Osdorp rampart near the Lauriergracht. The hairline cracks seen in the sky are probably the result of the etching ground cracking in the acid bath.

The inscription on the back of the second impression describes it as Rembrandt's grandfather's mill near Katwijk. However, that mill was actually quite different in appearance.

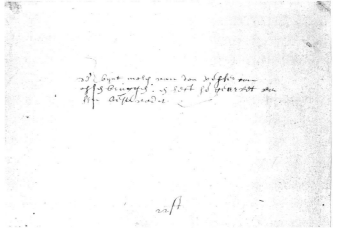

**B 234**

*View of Haarlem and Bloemendaal,* 1651
Etching and drypoint
Only state, 120 x 319 mm
Bottom left: Rembrandt f 1651

Here Rembrandt gives us a panorama of
the landscape behind the dunes seen from
a high viewpoint. On the left we see the
Saxenburg estate, which at this time
belonged to Rembrandt's creditor
Christoffel Thijsz. On the horizon to the
left the skyline of Haarlem can be seen
with the church of St. Bavo. In the right
middle ground, the steeple of
Bloemendaal.

**B 235**

*Landscape with an angler and two swans,*
1650
Etching and drypoint
State II (2), 82 x 107 mm
Bottom left: Rembrandt f 1650

**B 236**
*Landscape with a large boat,* 1650
Etching and drypoint
State II (2), 83 x 108 mm
Bottom left: Rembrandt. f. 1650

**B 237**
*Landscape with a cow,* c.1650
Etching and drypoint
State II (3), 103 x 130 mm
Since 1911 on loan from the
Rijksmuseum, Amsterdam

# Portraits

Portraits occupy an important place in Rembrandt's oeuvre. Even in his Leiden days he was already making studies of old men and women, for which his own parents would also doubtless have posed. These prints were probably not intended to be substantive works of art, but were rather Rembrandt's way of practising ways of depicting a range of facial expressions.

Between 1633 and 1664 Rembrandt made about twenty etched portraits. Most of them were not executed for commercial publication as prints or book illustrations, but were private prints made for personal reasons, though usually on commission. Many of those portrayed were acquaintances or friends.

The earliest portraits are fairly simple in conception and technique. The later portrait etchings are far more complex in composition and are detailed in a combination of techniques.

**B 259**
*Old man shading his eyes with his hand,*
c. 1639
Etching and drypoint
Only state, 138 x 115 mm

This etching was never finished: there are only a few lines to indicate the clothes and the chair.

**B 257**
*Man in an arbour,* 1642
Etching, only state, 72 x 56 mm
Top left: Rembrandt f 1642

**B 260**

*Old man looking down*, 1631
Etching, state II (3), 119 x 117 mm
Bottom right: RHL 1631

Like B 309 and B 325, this etching was
probably made from life or from one of
the drawings in red chalk that Rembrandt
made of old bearded men between 1630
and 1633.

**B 261**

*Man at a desk wearing a chain with a cross,*
1641
Etching and drypoint
State II (4), 154 x 102 mm
Bottom centre: Rembrandt f 1641

A conspicuous feature of this etching is
the sixteenth-century costume worn by
the young man. Rembrandt quite often
portrayed people wearing the dress of an
earlier period.

**B 262**
*Old man with a fur cap and a velvet cloak,*
c. 1632
Etching, state II (3), 149 x 130 mm
Left centre: RHL fe

**B 263**
*Man with oriental fur cap,* 1631
Etching and burin
State III (4), 145 x 129 mm
Top left: RHL 1631

**B 265**
*Old man wearing a divided fur cap*, 1640
Etching and drypoint
State II (2), 150 x 147 mm
Top left: Rembrandt f./ 1640

**B 264**
*Jan Antonides van der Linden, posthumous
portrait*, 1665
Etching, drypoint and burin
State V (5), 172 x 105 mm

Van der Linden (1609-1664) was a famous
physician who became professor of
medicine at Leiden in 1651. This etching,
as far as we know the last one Rembrandt
ever did, was made for the title-page of
the posthumous edition of van der
Linden's adaptations of Hippocrates.
However, the etching was never used for
this purpose because what the publisher
had actually ordered was an engraving.

**B 266**

*Jan Cornelis Sylvius*, 1633
Etching, state I (2), 166 x 141 mm
Left centre: Rembrandt/ f 1633

Jan Cornelis Sylvius (1564-1638) was from
1610 onwards a preacher of the Reformed
church in Amsterdam. When this etching
was made (1633) he was guardian of his
niece Saskia van Uylenburg, whom
Rembrandt was to marry in 1634.

**B 269**

*Samuel Manasseh ben Israel*, 1636
Etching, state III (3), 149 x 103 mm
Right centre: Rembrandt f/ 1636

Manasseh ben Israel (1604-1657) had fled
to Amsterdam from Portugal as a child
with his parents. At the age of eighteen he
was appointed a rabbi, but he was also a
printer of considerable note. In 1627 he
established the first printing house in
Amsterdam to produce editions of
religious works in Hebrew, Portuguese
and Spanish. For a while Manasseh lived
across the road from Rembrandt and they
would have known each other well. In
1655 Manasseh wrote a book called
'Piedra Gloriosa' which Rembrandt
illustrated with four etchings (B 36a-d).

**B 268**

*'Young man in a velvet cap'*
*The preacher Petrus Sylvius*, 1637
Etching, state II (2), 97 x 84 mm
Top left: Rembrandt/ f 1637

The identification of the sitter as Petrus
Sylvius appears to be the most convincing
(D. de Hoop Scheffer, 1974).
The preacher Petrus Sylvius (1610-1653)
was the son of Jan Cornelis Sylvius (B
266). Rembrandt made this portrait
shortly before Sylvius departed for Sloten
in Friesland, where he had been
appointed preacher.

**B 270**

*Faust*, c. 1652
Etching, drypoint and burin
State II (4), 210 x 160 mm

At the end of the seventeenth century this etching was still known as *The Practising Alchemist*; the title *Faust* dates from the eighteenth century.
The letters INRI stand for **I**esus **N**azarenus **R**ex **I**udaeorum (Jesus of Nazareth, king of the Jews): it is the text that Pilate had nailed to the Cross. The other letters in the ball of light form an anagram, the text of a prayer in reverse. The letters INRI and the anagram occur in exactly the same way on a seventeenth-century amulet. The composition appears to be based on two iconographical traditions: the scholar in an interior and the saint or evangelist surprised by a vision. (H. van de Waal, 1964)

**B 271**

*Cornelis Claesz. Anslo,* 1641
Etching and drypoint
State II (2), 108 x 158 mm
Right centre: Rembrandt. f./ 1641
Printed in the eighteenth century on
Japanese paper from the plate worked up
by Baillie

Anslo (1592-1646) was a cloth merchant in
Amsterdam and at the same time
preacher to the community of
Waterlanders in Amsterdam. The
Waterlanders were Mennonites, followers
of the Frisian anabaptist Menno Simonsz.
The picture was indented onto the etching
plate from a drawn study of 1640
(Benesch 758).

**B 272**

*Clement de Jonghe, printseller,* 1651
a) Etching, drypoint and burin
State I (6), 207 x 161 mm
Bottom right: Rembrandt f. 1651
b) Etching, drypoint and burin
State V (6), 207 x 161 mm
Bottom right: Rembrandt f. 1651

Clement de Jonghe was born in 1624/25 in
Schleswig-Holstein. In about 1656 he
moved to Amsterdam, where he worked
as a map-colourer, colouring and
decorating maps and charts. Later he
became a well-known publisher of prints
and maps. In 1679, two years after his
death, an inventory of his estate was
drawn up. The list includes a large
number of Rembrandt's etching plates,
which is how we know the titles by which
the etchings were known at the time.
The fifth state differs from the first in the
face and hat, in addition to which the
shadow passages are now much more
detailed. There is also a new archway
above the sitter.
Some authors dispute the identification. It
has been suggested that the subject is not
Clement de Jonghe but Jan Six
(J.R. Voûte, 1987).

**B 273**
*Abraham Francen, apothecary,* c. 1657
Etching, drypoint and burin
State IX (10), 158 x 108 mm
Late impression, probably eighteenth
century

Abraham Francen (1613-?) was a good
friend of Rembrandt's and acted as a
witness for him on a number of occasions.
He accepted the guardianship of
Cornelia, the daughter of Rembrandt and
Hendrickje Stoffels. Francen also was an
artcollector, and that is how Rembrandt
has depicted him here. This is
Rembrandt's only portrait-etching in
oblong format.

**B 275**
*Pieter Haaringh 'Young Haaringh'*, 1655
Etching, drypoint and burin
State II (5), 195 x 146 mm
Right centre: Rembrandt/ f. 1655
Since 1911 on loan from the
Rijksmuseum, Amsterdam

Pieter Haaringh (1609-1685) was from
1639 the Messenger (receiver) of the
orphans' court, in which capacity he
regulated all auctions not ordered by the
court. In 1655, i.e. before Rembrandt was
declared insolvent in 1656, Haaringh
auctioned some of his possessions for him.

**B 276**

*Jan Lutma, gold- and silversmith,* 1656
a) Etching and drypoint
State I (3), 196 x 150 mm
Top centre: Rembrandt/ f. 1656.
b) Etching, drypoint and burin
State II (3), 196 x 150 mm
Top centre: Rembrandt/ f. 1656.

Lutma (1584-1669) was born in Emden, Germany, but was entered as a citizen of Amsterdam in 1621. As a silversmith he was famous for his mastery of chasing. He worked mainly in the characteristic Auricular or Lobate style, also designing the choir screens for the Nieuwe Kerk in Amsterdam. Here we see him holding a piece of work in his hand. On the table beside him lie his tools: hammer and punches and a small silver dish.

a) The first state has been very lightly etched and then worked up with the drypoint. The impression is light silver-grey, probably the result of using very little ink. Rembrandt made 'silver prints' like this only of this one portrait.
b) In the second state a window and a recess in the wall have been added. An inscription has also been added, though not by Rembrandt.

**B 277**
*Jan Asselijn, painter,* c. 1647
Etching, drypoint and burin
State II (3), 216 x 170 mm
Bottom right: Rembr./ f. 16
Printed on Japanese paper

Jan Asselijn (*c.*1615-1652) was a landscape
painter. On account of a deformed hand
he was known as 'Krabbetje' - little crab.
After a period of several years in Rome he
came to Amsterdam in 1647, and it was at
about this time that Rembrandt made this
portrait of him.
In the first state of the print (plate 277A)
we see behind the painter an easel with
one of his Italianate landscapes.

plate 277A
Rembrandt, *Jan Asselijn*, state I (3),
Amsterdam, Rijksmuseum,
Rijksprentenkabinet.

## B 278

*Ephraim Bueno,* 1647
Etching, drypoint and burin
State II (2), 241 x 177 mm
Bottom right: Rembrandt f. 1647

Bueno (1559-1665), also known as Bonus, came from a well-known Portuguese Jewish family. He was a physician and a poet and translator into Spanish. He was also one of those who put up the money for Manasseh ben Israel's printing house, as well as being one of its customers. It was probably through Manasseh that he met Rembrandt.
The drypoint work may be seen particularly clearly in the velvety black of Bueno's cape.
This portrait etching is the only one for which a painted preliminary study exists (Bredius 252, plate 278A).

plate 278A
Rembrandt, *Ephraim Bueno,*
Amsterdam, Rijksmuseum.

**B 279**

*Jan Uytenbogaert*, 1635
Etching, drypoint and burin
State V (6), 250 x 187 mm
Top left: Rembrandt
Top right: 1635.

The preacher Uytenbogaert (1557-1644) was one of the leaders of the Arminians or Remonstrants, followers of Jacobus Arminius who believed in the more liberal religious tenets set out in the Remonstrance of 1610. However, the Synod of Dort (1618/19) removed all Arminians from their posts and sent many into exile. Uytenbogaert went to Antwerp but in 1626, thanks partly to the intercession of Prince Frederick Henry (whom he had once taught), he was able to return to The Hague.
This was Rembrandt's first official commission for an etched portrait. It is also one of his few portrait etchings to have a caption: a rather carelessly etched panegyric in Latin by Hugo Grotius, founder of modern public international law, the Arminians' most important political leader and a friend of Uytenbogaert's.

**B 281**

*Jan Uytenbogaert*, 1639
Etching and drypoint
State II (2), 250 x 204 mm
Bottom left: Rembrandt f./ 1639

This Jan Uytenbogaert (1608-1680), whose father was a cousin of the subject of B 279, studied in Leiden from 1626 until 1632. During that time he probably met Rembrandt, who was working there with Lievens. In 1632 Uytenbogaert became collector of taxes for the province of Holland. In 1639 he interceded on Rembrandt's behalf in the matter of payment for paintings commissioned by Frederick Henry, and it seems likely that this portrait is a mark of gratitude for his assistance.
The print shows Uytenbogaert, in sixteenth-century costume, weighing bags of money. In the eighteenth century the print acquired the familiar name *The Goldweigher*.

**B 282**
*Lieven Willemsz van Coppenol*, c. 1658
Etching, drypoint and burin
State III (6), 258 x 190 mm

Lieven van Coppenol (1598-after 1677)
was head of the so-called French school in
Amsterdam. In 1650 he fell prey to an
attack of insanity, after which he was no
longer allowed to teach. He then turned to
working as a professional calligrapher.
Rembrandt depicts Coppenol here just as
he has completed a freehand circle -
regarded as proof of competence with the
pen. The boy in the background is
Coppenol's grandson Andries.

**B 283**
*Lieven Willemsz van Coppenol*, 1658
Etching, drypoint and burin
State III (6), 341 x 290 mm
Since 1963 on loan from the
Rijksmuseum, Amsterdam

To distinguish it from the previous print,
this one is known as the 'large' Coppenol.
It is Rembrandt's largest etched portrait.

## B 285

*Portrait of Jan Six*, 1647
Etching, drypoint and burin
State IV (4), 245 x 191 mm
Bottom right: Rembrandt. f. 1647
Bottom left by Rembrandt:
JAN SIX.AE.29

Jan Six (1618-1700) was a scion of one of
the leading families of Amsterdam, where
he became a burgomaster (the city had
several) in 1691. His chief interest was in
the arts, especially poetry. Six and
Rembrandt probably first met in 1641.
For this etching Rembrandt did three
preliminary drawings, one of which was
indented onto the etching plate (Benesch
768, plate 285A). The print has been very
carefully executed. By judicious working
up of the etching with drypoint and burin
the artist has produced a rich pattern of
light and dark in the shadowy interior.
The plate from which this print was made
is still owned by the Six family.

plate 285A
Rembrandt, *Study for a portrait of Jan Six*,
Amsterdam, Six-collection.

**Bartsch 21**
**Jan Lievens** (1607-1674)
*Bust of an old man seen from the front*
Etching, state I (3), 160 x 143 mm
Left centre: IL (monograph); top right: 5
Haarlem, Teylers Museum

**B 286**
*The first 'oriental' head*, 1635
Etching and drypoint
State II (2), 151 x 125 mm
Top centre: Rembrandt geretuc/ 1635

**Four oriental heads**

Rembrandt made these four so-called oriental heads in 1635, modelling them on four etchings by Jan Lievens (Bartsch 21, 20, 18, 26). On the first three sheets Rembrandt wrote that he had 'retouched', i.e. improved, his examples. On the fourth he placed only his monogram.

It used to be thought that these prints were the work of a pupil and that Rembrandt had improved them. However, the current interpretation is that Rembrandt himself indented the outlines of Lievens's heads into the etching ground, then proceeding to fill in the details as he thought best - sometimes with quite different results.

**Bartsch 20**
**Jan Lievens**
*Bust of an old man wearing a fur cap*
Etching, state III (5), 164 x 144 mm
Bottom right: IL (monograph)/ Franc v
Wijngaerde ex.; top right: 3

**B 287**
*The second 'oriental' head,* 1635
Etching, only state, 151 x 125 mm
Top centre: Rembrandt geretuceert

**Bartsch 18**
**Jan Lievens**
*Bust of an old man wearing an turban*
Etching, state III (4), 146 x 126 mm
Right centre: 12
Haarlem, Teylers Museum

**B 288**
*The third 'oriental' head,* 1635
Etching, only state, 155 x 134 mm
Top left: Rembrandt geretuck/ .1635.

**Bartsch 26**
**Jan Lievens**
*Bust of a young man wearing a velvet beret*
Etching, state III (4), 146 x 126 mm
Right centre: 12

**B 289**
*The fourth 'oriental' head,* 1635
Etching, state II (2), 158 x 135 mm
Left centre: Rt

**B 290**
*Old man in a fur cap, with eyes closed,* c. 1635
Etching, only state, 112 x 101 mm
Top left: R (reversed)/Rembrandt

**B 291**
*Bearded old man, with white sleeve,* c. 1631
Etching, only state, 71 x 64 mm

This bust is virtually identical to the upper part of a portrait of an old man drawn at about the same time in red chalk (Benesch 41, plate 291A). There are indentation marks all over the drawing, but there is no known etching of the whole figure.

plate 291A
Rembrandt, *Old man seated,*
Berlijn, S.M.P.K., Kupferstichkabinett.

**B 294**
*Bald-headed man in profile (Rembrandt's father?)*, 1630
Etching, only state, 57 x 43 mm
Top left: RL/1630

For commentary see B 292.

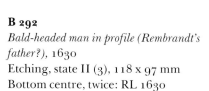

**B 292**
*Bald-headed man in profile (Rembrandt's father?)*, 1630
Etching, state II (3), 118 x 97 mm
Bottom centre, twice: RL 1630

There is no hard evidence to support the traditional identification of this model as Rembrandt's father. The same man also appears in B 263, B 294 and B 321.

**B 305**
**Unknown pupil of Rembrandt**
*Curly-headed man with a wry mouth*
Etching, state I (2), 64 x 60 mm

**B 310**
*Portrait of a boy, in profile,*
*(Prince Willem II?),* 1641
Etching, only state, 93 x 67 mm
Top right: Rembrandt. f 1641

The boy's face is reminiscent of an
engraved portrait of Prince William II by
W. Delff. However, by the time
Rembrandt made this little portrait the
prince (1625-50) had already reached the
age of 16 and the model appears to be
considerably younger than that.

**B 309**
*Old man with a flowing beard,* 1630
Etching, only state, 98 x 81 mm
Top left: RHL 1630

**B 311**
*Man in a broad-brimmed hat,* 1638(?)
Etching, only state, 79 x 64 mm
Top left: RHL/ 1638

After 1633 this is the only occurrence of
the monogram RHL. It is possible that the
signature and date are not autographs.

**B 312**
*Old man with a fur cap and flowing beard,*
1631
Etching, state II (2) 62 x 54 mm

**B 321**
*Man wearing a high cap,*
*(Rembrandt's father?),* 1630
a) Etching, state II (2), 102 x 84 mm
Top left: RL 1630
b) Counterproof of state II
For an explanation of the technique
see p. 15
Since 1948 on loan from a private
collection

For commentary see B 292.

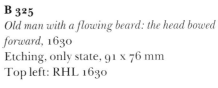

**B 325**
*Old man with a flowing beard: the head bowed*
*forward,* 1630
Etching, only state, 91 x 76 mm
Top left: RHL 1630

For commentary see B 260.

**B 313**
*Man in a velvet cap with a jewel clasp,* 1637
Etching, only state, 95 x 82 mm
Top left: Rembrandt/ f. 1637

**B 316** and **B 320**
See page 34

**B 340**
*Esther before her visit to Ahasverus,*
*(the great Jewish bride)*, 1635
Etching, drypoint and burin
State V (5), 219 x 168 mm
Top right: R 1635 (in reverse)

The eighteenth-century collector Valerius
Röver gave this print the title 'The great
Jewish bride', but modern opinion is that
this is the Biblical figure Esther, preparing
for her audience with King Ahasuerus to
plead on behalf of the Jews living in
Persia. In her left hand she holds the
decree ordering their extermination
(Esther 4:15-17). A painterly effect is
achieved by the careful representation of
hair and garments and the balanced
contrasts of light and dark.

**B 343**
*Rembrandt's mother seated at a table*, c. 1631
Etching, state II (3), 149 x 131 mm
Left centre: RHL. f.

Neeltgen Willemsdochter van Zuytbroeck
(1568-1640) had ten children of whom
Rembrandt was the last but one. She came
from a Leiden family of some standing.
Documentary confirmation of the identity
of this model has yet to be found, but the
portrait is referred to in this way as early
as·the inventory of the print dealer
Clement de Jonghe (see B 272) of 1679.
Rembrandt depicted the same woman in
B 344, 348, 351, 352 and 354, and in a
number of paintings.

**B 344**
**Unknown pupil of Rembrandt**
*Rembrandts mother in widow's dress*, c. 1635
Etching, only state, 150 x 117 mm
Top left: Rembrandt/ f. (by another hand)

**B 350**
*Old woman sleeping*, c. 1635/37
Etching, only state, 69 x 52 mm

**B 345**
*Woman reading*, 1634
Etching, state II (3), 123 x 100 mm
Top centre: Rembrandt. f 1634.

**B 347**
*Saskia with pearls in her hair*, 1634
Etching, only state, 87 x 68 mm
Top centre: Rembrandt f./ 1634

Saskia van Uylenburgh and Rembrandt
married in 1634 in Friesland; in the same
year Rembrandt made this dreamy,
sophisticated portrait of his wife.

**B 352**
*Rembrandt's mother, full face*, 1628
Etching, state II (2), 63 x 64 mm
Left centre: RHL 1628 ('2' in reverse)

For Rembrandt's portraits of his mother,
see commentary to B 343.

**B 351**
*Rembrandt's mother in a cloth headdress*, 1633
Etching, state II (2), 42 x 40 mm
Top centre: Rembrandt. f. 1633

For Rembrandt's portraits of his mother,
see commentary to B 343.

**B 354**
*Bust of Rembrandt's mother*, 1628
Etching, state II (2), 65 x 63 mm
Top right: RHL 1628 ('2' in reverse)

For Rembrandt's portraits of his mother,
see commentary to B 343.

**B 357**
*The white negress*, c. 1630
Etching, state II (2), 98 x 77 mm

**B 356**
*Girl with a basket*, c. 1642
Etching, state II (2), 87 x 60 mm

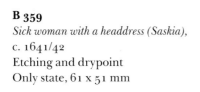

**B 359**
*Sick woman with a headdress (Saskia)*,
c. 1641/42
Etching and drypoint
Only state, 61 x 51 mm

# Sheets of studies

In a number of sheets of sketches, most of them executed between 1632 and 1638, Rembrandt used the etching plate like a leaf out of a sketchbook. They contain various motifs, such as portraits (often of Saskia) and studies of peasants and beggars. Each plate has been used at several different angles. In the grouping of the figures on the page and in the playful, drawing-like flow of the lines, these etchings look much like the drawn sketch-leaves of the same period, e.g. plate 365A.

plate 365A
Rembrandt, *Four studies of Saskia and Rombertus*,
Rotterdam, Museum Boymans-van Beuningen.

**B 363**
*Sheet of studies: self-portrait, a beggar couple,*
*heads of an old man and old woman, etc.,*
c. 1632
Etching, state II (2), 100 x 105 mm

**B 365**

*Five studies of the head of Saskia, and one of an older woman*, 1636
Etching, only state, 151 x 126 mm
Bottom centre: Rembrandt. f/ 1636

This sheet of studies contains five studies of Saskia and top left, a portrait of another, older woman. The manner of working, with fine, carefully drawn lines, is related to the style of a drawn sheet of studies (plate 365A, p. 169). On both sheets Saskia is wearing the same kind of hat.

**B 367**

*Three heads of women, probably all Saskia*, c.1637
Etching, state III (3), 127 x 103 mm

**B 368**
*Three heads of women: one asleep,* 1637
Etching, only state, 143 x 97 mm
Top centre: Rembrandt/ f 1637

The woman depicted twice on the right is
probably Saskia again.

**B 369**

*Sheet of studies, with a woman lying ill in bed, a beggar couple, and several old men,* c. 1641/42
Etching, only state, 151 x 136 mm

The woman in bed, who appears twice on this sheet, is probably Saskia. She died in 1642 after a long illness.

**B 372**
*Sheet of studies: with upper part of a self-portrait and a tree,* c. 1638
Etching, only state, 78 x 69 mm

**B 370**
*Sheet of studies with self-portrait, a beggar man, woman and child,* 1651
Etching, only state, 111 x 92 mm
Bottom right: RL 1651
(possibly not autographic)

# Abbreviated list of literature

BARTSCH 1797
A. Bartsch, *Catalogue raisonné de toutes les estampes qui forment l'oeuvre de Rembrandt*, Vienna 1797.

BARTSCH 1803-1821
A. Bartsch, *Le peintre-graveur*, 21 vols, Vienna 1797.

BENESCH 1953-1957
O. Benesch, *The drawings of Rembrandt*, 6 vols.; London/New York 1953-1957; enlarged and edited by Eva Benesch, London and New York 1973.

BIÖRKLUND 1968
G. Biörklund and O.H. Barnard, *Rembrandt's Etchings True and False*, 2nd edition, London, Stockholm and New York 1968.

BOON 1963
K.G. Boon, *Rembrandt: The Complete Etchings*, New York 1963.

BREDIUS 1935
A. Bredius, *Rembrandt. The Complete Edition of the Paintings*, Utrecht 1935, revised edition by H. Gerson, London 1969.

BRUYN 1959
J. Bruyn, *Rembrandts keuze van bijbelse onderwerpen*, Utrecht 1959.

CAMPBELL 1980
C. Campbell, 'Rembrandts etsen *Het sterfbed va Maria* en *De drie bomen*', *Kroniek van het Rembrandthuis*, 1980, vol 2, pp. 2-33.

FILEDT KOK 1972
J.P. Filedt Kok, *Rembrandt etchings and drawings in the Rembrandt House*, Maarssen 1972.

GERSAINT 1751
E.F. Gersaint, *Catalogue raisonné de toutes les pièces qui forment l'oeuvre de Rembrandt*, Paris 1751.

GROOT, DE 1979
I. de Groot, *Landscape Etchings by the Dutch Masters of the seventeenth century*, Maarssen 1979.

HAAK 1968
B. Haak, *Rembrandt: His Life, His Work, His Time*, New York 1969.

HIND 1923
A.M. Hind, *A Catalogue of Rembrandt's Etchings*, London 1923, 2nd edition, 2 vols., reprinted in one vol., New York 1967.

HOLLSTEIN 1949-
F.W.H. Hollstein, *Dutch and Flemish Etchings, Engravings and Woodcuts, c. 1450-1700*, Amsterdam 1949-

HOOP SCHEFFER, DE, 1974
D. de Hoop Scheffer, 'Petrus Sylvius par Rembrandt', in: *Liber Amicorum Karel G. Boon*, Amsterdam 1974, pp. 94-101.

KISCH 1984
M. Royalton-Kisch, 'Over Rembrandt en van Vliet', *Kroniek van het Rembrandthuis*, 1984, vol 1-2, pp. 3-23.

LUGT 1915
F. Lugt, *Wandelingen met Rembrandt in en om Amsterdam*, Amsterdam 1915.

MUNZ 1952
L. Münz, *Rembrandt's etchings*, 2 vols., London 1952.

SCHWARTZ 1977
G. Schwartz, *Rembrandt. All the etchings of Rembrandt reproduced in true size*, Maarssen 1977.

STRAUSS 1979
W.L. Strauss and M. van der Meulen, *The Rembrandt documents*, New York 1979.

SUMOWSKI 1979-1985
W. Sumowski, *Drawings of the Rembrandt School*, 9 vols., New York 1979-1985.

TÜMPEL 1974
A. Tümpel, 'Claes Cornelisz. Moeyart'. *Oud Holland* 88, 1974, pp. 47 ff.

VOÛTE 1987
J.R. Voûte, 'Clement de Jonghe exit', *Kroniek van het Rembrandthuis*, 1987, vol 1, pp. 21-27.

WAAL, VAN DE 1964
H. van de Waal, 'Rembrandt's Faust etching. A Socinian document and the iconography of the inspired scholar', *Oud Holland*, 1964, pp. 1-48.

WHITE 1969
C. White, *Rembrandt as an etcher*, London 1969.

WHITE 1970
C. White and K.G. Boon, *Rembrandt's Etchings: An Illustrated Critical Catalogue*, 2 vols., Amsterdam and New York 1970. (Compilation of vols. XVII and XVIII of F.W.H. Hollstein, *Dutch and Flemish Etchings, Engravings and Woodcuts, c. 1450-1700*, Amsterdam 1949-)

## Catalogues

**Amsterdam 1976**
**E. de Jongh,** *tot Lering en Vermaak*, Rijksmuseum, Amsterdam 1976.

**Amsterdam 1977**
*The Dutch Cityscape and its Sources*, Amsterdams Historisch Museum 1977; Art Gallery of Toronto 1977.

**Amsterdam 1981**
E. Ornstein-van Slooten, *Work in Process. Rembrandt etchings in different states*, Museum het Rembrandthuis 1981.

**Amsterdam 1982**
P. Schatborn, *Dutch Figure Drawings from the seventeenth century*, Rijksprentenkabinet, Rijksmuseum 1982; National Gallery of Art, Washington 1982.

**Amsterdam 1983**
P. Schatborn, *Landscapes by Rembrandt and his precursors*, Museum het Rembrandthuis 1983.

**Amsterdam 1984-1985**
P. Schatborn and E. Ornstein-van Slooten, *Rembrandt as teacher*, Museum het Rembrandthuis 1984-1985.

**Amsterdam 1985-1986**
B. Broos, *Rembrandt and his sources*, Museum het Rembrandthuis 1985-1986.

**Amsterdam 1986-1987**
R.E.O. Ekkart and E. Ornstein-van Slooten, *Face to face with the sitters for Rembrandt's etched portraits*, Museum het Rembrandthuis 1986-1987.

**Amsterdam 1987-1988**
S.A.C. Dudok van Heel, E. Ornstein-van Slooten and P. Schatborn, *The Rembrandt papers. Documents, drawings and prints*, Museum het Rembrandthuis 1987-1988.

**Amsterdam 1988-1989**
P. Schatborn and E. Ornstein-van Slooten, *Jan Lievens. Prints and drawings*, Museum het Rembrandthuis 1988-1989.

**Berlijn 1970**
C. en A. Tümpel, *Rembrandt legt die Bibel aus*, Staatliche Museen, Berlijn 1970

**Boston 1969**
*Rembrandt. Experimental Etcher*, Museum of Fine Arts 1969; Piermont Morgan Library, New York 1969-1970.

**Boston 1980-1981**
C.S. Ackley, *Printmaking in the Age of Rembrandt*, Museum of Fine Arts 1980-1981; Saint Louis Art Museum 1980-1981.

**Chicago 1969-1970**
*Rembrandt after Three Hundred Years*, The Art Institute of Chicago 1969-1970; Minneapolis Institute of Arts 1969-1970; The Detroit Institute of Arts 1969-1970.

**London 1969**
*The Late Etchings of Rembrandt*, British Museum 1969.

**Paris 1986**
S. de la Bussière, *Rembrandt Eaux-Fortes*, Musée du Petit Palais 1986.

**Rome 1951**
J.Q. van Regteren Altena, *Mostra di incisioni e disegni di Rembrandt*, Palazzo Venezia 1951; Gabinetto delle Stampe e dei Disegni della Galleria degli Uffizi, Florence 1951.

**Vienna 1970-1971**
*Rembrandts Radierungen aus dem Besitz der Albertina*, Albertina 1970-1971.

**Washington 1990**
C.P. Schneider and others, *Rembrandt's Landscapes. Drawings and Prints*, National Gallery of Art 1990.

## Colofon

*Publisher:* Waanders Publishers, Zwolle
*Design:* Roelof Koebrugge bNO
*Printing:* Waanders Printers, Zwolle

© 1991   Uitgeverij Waanders b.v., Zwolle
Museum Het Rembrandthuis, Amsterdam
All rights reserved. No part of this publication may be rereproduced, stored in a retrieval system, or transmitted in any form or by any means, electronic, photocopying, recording, or otherwise, without prior permission, in writing, from the publishers.

**Sources of illustrations**
The photographs were provided by the owners of the works reproduced.

Cip-gegevens Koninklijke Bibliotheek, Den Haag

Ornstein-Van Slooten, Eva

The Rembrandthuis: the prints, drawings and paintings / Eva Ornstein-Van Slooten, Marijke Holtrop, Peter Schatborn - Zwolle : Waanders. - ill.
ISBN 90-6630-233-X
NUGI 911/921
Trefw.:Rembrandt / prentkunst ; Nederland ; geschiedenis ; 17e eeuw.